FAST

BROKE

Learn the real reason athletes

go broke -

so you don't have to

By Danny Schayes

Copyright © 2014 **Danny Schayes**

Published by *Nomad CEO Publishing*

ISBN-13:978-1502869715

Legal Disclaimer

All Rights Reserved. No part of this publication may be reproduced in any form or by any means, including scanning, photocopying, or otherwise without prior written permission of the copyright holder.

Disclaimer and Terms of Use: The Author and Publisher has strived to be as accurate and complete as possible in the creation of this book, notwithstanding the fact that he does not warrant or represent at any time that the contents within are accurate due to the rapidly changing nature of the Internet. While all attempts have been made to verify information provided in this publication, the Author and Publisher assumes no responsibility for errors, omissions, or contrary interpretation of the subject matter herein. Any perceived slights of specific persons, peoples, or organizations are unintentional. In practical advice books, like anything else in life, there are no guarantees of income made. Readers are cautioned to rely on their own judgment about their individual circumstances to act accordingly. This book is not intended for use as a source of legal, business, accounting or financial advice. All readers are advised to seek services of competent professionals in the legal, business, accounting, and finance fields.

Fast Broke

Dedication

To Wendy, Thanks for being on the planet, encouraging everyone to be their best!

To Logan, I get to enjoy being a kid all over again. Thanks for showing up when you did.

Fast Broke

Fast Broke

Acknowledgements

I want to thank some of the many people who made a difference in my life and my education. First and most, my wife Wendy, who insists that everyone around her honor their potential. It doesn't always make her popular, but it always makes her amazing. I also want to thank my parents, Dolph and Naomi Schayes. They were always there for me and stepped up the most when things were the worst.

To my friends Cathy Reece, Anthony Austin and John Balitis: Thanks for proving that when things go south, there are honorable folks who step up to make the difference, even if it means going beyond what's reasonable.

To the people who showed me the way and provided the lessons that I needed at the time, I appreciate all that you taught me. Thanks to Robert Kiyosaki, Ken McElroy, Lou Brown, Will "Power" Duquette, Marshall Sylver, Tom Wheelright, Scott Snow, Marshall Thurber and Landmark Education. You each gave generously of your time and energy.

And a special thanks to Dr. Ei-ichi Negishi, the educator who made such an impact on a young student so many years ago. Even after 35 years, I still appreciate so many of the things that you taught me and remember how much you believed in me. Congratulations on winning the Nobel Prize. It couldn't have happened to a nicer guy.

Fast Broke

Fast Broke

Table of Contents

Acknowledgements v

Introduction ix

Chapter 1: Why Athletes Fail
(and why you probably will, too) 1

Chapter 2: Smart Money vs. Dumb Money 11

Chapter 3: Starting Out 23

Chapter 4: Learning the Basics 27

Chapter 5: Left Foot First 35

Chapter 6: It's In No One's Interest That You Get It! 39

Chapter 7: My Awakening 47

Chapter 8: How To Go Broke on $100 Million 53

Chapter 9: You Were The Best There Is, So What's Next? ... 65

Chapter 10: The Spam Hits The Fan 73

Chapter 11: Create A Structure To Use 77

Chapter 12: Most People Come From Lack, Not Abundance ... 85

Chapter 13: Always Know The Score 95

Chapter 14: Everyone Has A Coach 101

Epilogue 111

About The Author 113

Fast Broke

Fast Broke

Introduction

During my 18-year NBA career, I tried many different strategies to become financially free. I learned about finance, hired quality advisors, created investment plans and saved as much money as I could to feed my plan. All of these actions were taken with the deliberate intentions to attain my financial goals.

The problem was that after all of that time and effort, what I ended up with was money in the bank (my savings), little income and none of the financial freedom for which I had worked so long and hard.

What happened? What had gone wrong?

After studying on it for a long time I realized that I had little to no chance of meeting my financial goals because the system did not exist to achieve that. As a matter of fact, the only system that existed was the one that separated a player from his money, not helped it grow. To be successful, a player had to figure it out for himself against great odds.

I started this quest to create the system that I wanted to exist when I was a player. I am a win-win guy. I could easily envision a system where advisors made a lot by helping the players make even more. After all, there is no better salesman than a successful client.

So why didn't this system exist already? Why did I have such a hard time finding the answers?

I found out that I was my own answer. I would not find financial freedom until I deserved it, by respecting money and understanding how it really worked. Only then would I make the right choices that would lead to my desired outcome.

Fast Broke

I am a big believer that we generally make the choices that support what we are trying to accomplish. The hard part is truly understanding what that is. Most of us are so driven by our subconscious programming that we make decisions without really understanding what drives us.

The other problem most of us face is the lack of clarity to create a working structure that supports success.

The goal of this book is to provide a look into the world in which athletes live to see both of these factors at work. By viewing the process that athletes use to succeed and fail, we can all see ourselves in their "mirror," providing a clear picture of the forces that operate in our lives that keep us from enjoying the success we deserve.

Then I provide a detailed look into the most understandable and proven success model ever created. The model is how athletes and teams succeed in professional sports. Whether you are an athlete yourself or just someone wanting to get great results, you will experience how easy it is to see your way clearly.

I am convinced that you will get tremendous value from this book. It is the product of much research and experimentation. By truly understanding the forces at work in your life, you will be able to see a clear path to what you want.

Enjoy!

Danny Schayes

CHAPTER 1

Why Athletes Fail
(and why you probably will, too)

We have all seen the statistics and heard the stories about the majority of athletes going broke soon after they retire, regardless of how much money they made. I have this discussion with many people - especially athletes – on why this happens. The truth is very different than what many people think it is. I will discuss the mechanism at length later in this book, but the truth itself is simple. The reason that many athletes fail financially is the same reason that the vast majority of working people fail financially in retirement.

The system is designed for you to fail!

In Chapter 6 I will show you how the system uses many tricks to keep you confused, poorly educated and dependent on others. I will then demonstrate many of the traps that have been perfected to separate highly paid athletes from their money so you can see these same devices operating in your life.

And lastly, I will teach you how to create an effective system to become educated, create clarity in your life and regularly generate effective results.

The stories of athletes "blowing their money" seem entertaining on the surface. The reality is that it happens in a systematic way that can affect you as well. The lessons you will learn from the athlete experience will provide the roadmap for you to achieve the success that probably has eluded you until now.

Did you hear the joke about the optimist who jumped off the Empire

Fast Broke

State Building? As he was passing the 50th floor, someone with an open window heard him say, "Well so far, so good!" While that joke is great for a laugh, it also sums up the problem that many athletes - and working people - have planning for retirement. Think about the person in the joke. At the 50th floor, all he sees is an awesome view. He knows that the end will come eventually, but for now, he still has a long way to go.

Even when he sees the bottom, it is difficult to comprehend the inevitable "splat." It is still too far away to seem worrisome. The athlete's career is such an exaggeration of "real life" that it is difficult for him to relate to his upcoming fate.

At the end of a playing career, an athlete has come off a long period of high focus, perhaps as much as two decades and certainly all of his adult life to that point. He has committed his life to daily excellence at his chosen field. He has had a great deal of success. He has had a wonderful time "off the court" with the prestige, tremendous public presence and adoration and fan support of potentially millions of people. And he has been showered with millions of dollars for the privilege.

Not a bad life for someone who probably had little income earning potential otherwise. Statistically, there is a less than 30 percent chance that he graduated from college. He has an even lower chance of being a serious student. Without sports, his ability to step into a six-figure salary is practically zero. Yet here he is with a seven-figure salary without having the first clue as to what to do with it. Sports and entertainment have the highest discrepancy between the amount of money performers make and the level of business education needed to make it. Even Internet millionaires need to know how to run a business before they take their companies public for huge paydays.

Fast Broke

But what is there for athletes to know? Paychecks keep coming. There is always more. For the first time in their lives, they can have whatever they want. The ease of financial success can easily seduce the player. After all, while he worked extremely hard for years to perfect his athletic skill, he hasn't spent much time (if any) learning his financial skill.

And yet here he is, making a salary equivalent to the CEO of a billion-dollar company. Pro sports are one of the few areas where a player can earn a ton of money without knowing the first thing about finance.

Why athletes are just an exaggerated version of you

The more I talk to people in conventional careers, the more I hear about their feelings about athletes' inability to hang on to their money. I hear a wide range of opinions - all negative - usually describing the different types of stupidity of the various athletes and the things that are typically reported in the media about financial failures among athletes. I virtually never get any opinion from a non-athlete that any of these stories relate in any way to people in "real life."

I find it fascinating that so few people can relate their own financial difficulties or mistakes to what they read about in the media. I love having this conversation when people can finally see themselves as a smaller version of the athlete.

I usually start by discussing the actual issues at work versus some of the absurd examples in the media. While there are certainly cases of athletes blowing all of their money on strippers, cars and other frivolous items, the vast majority follow a very different path. Most are decent savers who want to do the right thing. They hold the majority of their wealth in cash. They don't know how to earn income from holdings, so they become dependent on "advisors." I go through a detailed examination of why athletes typically go broke later in this book.

But that doesn't change the fact that for most of the public, the prevailing issue that arises first is the perception that athletes buy a lot of stuff. We all read the stories of the guy with 50 suits, tons of jewelry, multiple cars, or some other seemingly ridiculous lifestyle item.

On a larger scale, an athlete's spending habits are not much different than those of non-athletes. The vast majority of Americans, as you know, spend much more than they make and often buy totally unnecessary items.

This is a result of the millions of advertising messages constantly forced upon us. As a society, we are urged at every opportunity to buy stuff we don't need, more than we can easily afford, and do it often. We have credit cards stuffed in our wallets and become slaves to them. Our entire society is stressed by money problems, and then we are surprised that athletes with gobs of money buy tons of stuff. After all, don't you want to keep up with the Kardashians?

I then ask about other issues that "plague" athletes. Let's look at some of the typical items:

- Family needs – parents and relatives needing help
- Peer pressure
- Friends in need – getting hit up for help
- Wanting to give your kids everything
- Losing your job and needing to feed your lifestyle
- Unprepared to make important money decisions

Fast Broke

> ➤ Understanding business on a high level

None of these issues are unique to athletes at all; they are universal. The only thing that makes athletes' experiences different is the scale. The reason I believe that athletes are such a good example to study is because their lives are (a) lived very much in the public eye and (b) merely an exaggerated version of what many people face every day.

By studying and understanding what athletes face, there is much to learn about how you can do better in handling your own situation. I think you will have a lot of fun peeking behind the curtain of athletes' lives. By seeing what athletes do wrong - and also what they do right - you will be able to see yourself much more clearly.

That is why it is so important to look beyond the obvious and really see what forces are at work. I am totally convinced that these same forces are at work in your life as well.

One of the obvious features about athletes and entertainers is the massive gap between the amount of money they earn and the level of financial education they have to earn that money. Remember, the income level that professional athletes achieve is on par with captains of industry, major Wall Street executives and CEOs of international companies.

These other individuals all have extensive formal education, years of real world financial experience, and large trusted support staffs of accountants, attorneys and business managers. These executives have access to the finest money managers and investment products. But most importantly, they have the mindset of a wealthy person. What I mean by that is they have been taught the elements of wealth building.

Fast Broke

Here's another joke: "What do you get when you give a poor person a lot of money?" The answer is, of course, "A poor person." The fact that a player has been given a fish - even one as big as a whale - doesn't give him the ability to fish, especially when he enters waters filled with ravenous sharks that are much better at getting it from him than he is at keeping it. The fact that a person has eye-popping athletic skills does not translate one iota into being a disciplined financial manager. The skill, mindset and disciplines are completely different and need to be learned, as I found out.

What does this all mean for you? Keep in mind that if you are in a field that is not financial in nature, you will also find yourself in the position of entering the shark-filled waters of the institutions: banks, insurance companies and mutual fund companies.

All have highly trained armies of salespeople who seem well meaning and are sharing wealth strategies that involve you giving them your money, on a regular and ongoing basis, and locking it up for years and years. It usually comes with a penalty for removing it, with virtually all of the risk on your side.

The information these institutions give you is typically designed to make them a lot of money while returning you very little, all while making it seem like a really good deal for you. They will make it seem complicated enough that you resist doing it yourself and leave it up to them to handle for you. It is easy to see why so many people who are windfall earners have such trouble keeping it together, especially at the beginning.

Imagine being a 16-year-old kid who learning to drive. You take a few lessons and get your driver's license. Now you are driving on your own, but your first car is a Lamborghini. Remember, we are talking about someone receiving large amounts of money without the skill to manage it. Our analogy is a kid getting a sports car without the skill to handle it.

So what do you think happens? More than likely, he crashes the Lamborghini. He is in over his head and lacks both the training and experience to handle the power he has been given.

Remember our kid has had some driving lessons but lacks the experience to know what real life driving is like in all conditions. He lacks the experience to understand driving in bad weather (investing in a rough or volatile market). He doesn't know the advanced skills that keep him safe in heavy traffic or an emergency situation (dealing with an investment going against him). And most importantly, he doesn't understand the risk of having something terrible happen (causing an accident, driving under the influence, texting while driving) and the awful, lasting consequences of making bad decisions. So if you give an inexperienced driver a Lamborghini, you can expect something bad will happen. Sooner or later, he will crash.

It's the same with money. When you give a young person with little experience or foundation a lot of money, you can expect that a large percentage of the time he will make choices not in his long-term best interest, and bad things will happen.

Now add to this equation the fact that he is surrounded by folks who are trained to get as much of that money as they can. At the end of the day, it's not at all surprising that athletes wind up with disappointing results when it comes to finances. I will discuss these mechanisms in detail later in the book. Remember to examine your own financial world and see how familiar it probably is.

Fast Broke

So why is a poor person given a lot of money still a poor person? To really get the point, it is important to examine the mindset of a poor person.

A poor person's entire life has been from a place of lack. They never had enough of anything or any surplus. At the same time, they were bombarded with millions of messages about buying all of the cool stuff you see on TV. They were constantly fed images of celebrities, rap artists, athletes and musicians and all of their big, expensive, cool stuff. MTV had a show "Cribs" that toured celebrity mansions. Most rap stars are drowning in gold, jewels and Bentleys and talk about throwing money around. The primary message is that money has one purpose: You buy stuff with it.

It is extremely rare for a young person coming from lack to have any other idea about money. How can you expect an instant millionaire who came from nothing, surrounded by people who are broke, to think about the dynamics of investments, passive income, or any other financial planning concept? It doesn't compute. These concepts never hit the radar. And frankly, it is the same for most people.

How else can you explain the statistics that show the vast majority of people need to work well past retirement age? Until a person can transform that truth about money and see another use for it, there is little chance for a successful outcome, *no matter how much they make.*

Typically, athletes are incapable of comprehending this notion for the first year or two of their careers. They need to satisfy that buying urge before they can even hear about something else. This is pretty universal, whether you are a successful athlete or not.

Not many folks of any circumstance start putting money away from

Fast Broke

their first paycheck. And in reality, this is the time when you have no stuff and need to fill your life with necessary items. You need a place to live and furniture, TVs, appliances, pots and pans and other items that make a place livable. You need a car, clothes, a computer, etc.

It is nearly impossible to start saving before this happens.

Furthermore, you have your whole life ahead of you and it is natural to leave the long-term stuff for another day. The money is burning a hole in your pocket. Believe me, I had a list of my own stuff to get. In a strange way, I was fortunate that upon entering the NBA, I didn't make enough money to go overboard. I already had my used car from college, so I had a little time before I needed a new ride. I had a rented house and was single, so my domestic needs were modest. I had the typical bare-bones place of a young man in his twenties.

My first major adult purchase was the result of extreme necessity: a washer and dryer. Really! I was in a hotel for training camp and I went to the laundromat to wash my clothes. Once. That was all it took. The day I moved into my rented house, I drove directly to Sears and had them deliver my new washer and dryer. Boy, did I feel like a king. I could wash my own clothes at home. I was living large!

I guess we each have our own needs.

Fast Broke

Fast Broke

Chapter 2

Smart Money vs. Dumb Money

"A fool and his money is one big party!"

If you read only one chapter in this book, read this one. It has the answer why so few succeed while most fail miserably.

We have all heard that athletes and entertainers blow all of their money on cars, drugs, jewelry, clothes and women, and not necessarily in that order. We hear every day about all these poor slobs who burn through millions of dollars and are left broke and lonely with no friends or opportunities. They live the obscene high life for a while. But when the money runs out, the friends run out, and the fun runs out. What happened? How is it possible to go through all that money? The answer is simpler than you think.

As we look at the person known to investors as "Dumb Money," we will see why it is the rule rather than the exception. In addition, hopefully you will understand how everyone lives some form of a "Dumb Money" lifestyle and how you can learn from the mistakes of others, rather than your own.

"Dumb Money" is a simple concept. The term refers to anyone who buys liabilities rather than assets. Many of these liabilities are disguised as "investments." Financial choices are driven more by ego and instant gratification than by design and the need for long-term results. So what does it mean to buy a liability instead of an asset? A liability is anything that costs more than it makes. It can be something you consume (clothes, trips, food, etc.) or something that has depreciating value (jewelry, cars, negative cash flow real estate, etc.). The term is mostly applied to people who buy or invest in things that they know little or nothing about. They are dependent on others to explain it to them and manage it. They don't understand what it is or how it works. And most importantly, if it fell to them to manage, they would be totally lost and helpless.

Most investors at all levels fall into the category of "Dumb Money." They need stockbrokers to pick their stocks. Few have any idea about the companies in which they "invest." They pour money into mutual funds without the first clue what is in them.

What excuse do you use for this type of investing?

"Who has the time?"

"It's too complicated."

"I'm supposed to own stocks, aren't I?"

These are just a few of the reasons that most people use.

How many real estate investors really know about the risks of owning rental properties? They went to a seminar, or listened to a friend, or know a realtor and – as Los Angeles Clippers announcer Ralph Lawler would say – Bingo! They are a real estate investor! Then they try to fix it, rent it, flip it or something else and learn that the market didn't do what it was supposed to do.

Or they might have had the worst possible thing happen: *They made money the first time but didn't know how they did it.* This is the ultimate recipe for disaster, because you fall into the trap of believing that you know what you are doing or that it is easy. You follow the trail of easy success and get in deeper and deeper until the market goes against you and you don't know how to fix the deal or trade. That is when the big fly swatter of life crashes down and you learn what it means to be "Dumb Money."

Smart Money

"Smart Money," on the other hand, is much more valuable to the success of any investment. "Smart Money" is the combination of capital and the good judgment of the person or entity controlling it. It brings together the value of the money in making a deal happen, with the additional value of advice and connections.

One of the places that you see the value of Smart Money is on the hit TV show "Shark Tank." On this show, ordinary entrepreneurs pitch their investment ideas to a panel of extraordinarily successful businessmen and women – including Dallas Mavericks owner Mark Cuban - in an attempt to secure investment from the "sharks." More often than not, the real value of the partnerships is to match a hard-working entrepreneur who has a great product with a partner who can supply "Smart Money." Rarely is the money the real benefit for the entrepreneur. The more important element is the ability of the "shark" to add value by using his business acumen and contacts to get the product on QVC, build a brand, provide legal support or possibly set up manufacturing. The key is that it takes a lot more than money to make a business successful. "Smart Money" makes sound choices about where to invest, then adds greater value in the ability to make a deal prosper.

The goal of any investor - especially an athlete - is to make the transition from "Dumb Money" to "Smart Money." It is not an easy thing to do, for several reasons. The first is the complete mental shift that has to take place. Another major reason is that successful investors are notoriously tight with their information. It takes a great

Fast Broke

deal of effort and determination to gain access to a highly successful investor in any meaningful way. There is obviously a tremendous amount of information available in print, on the web or in seminar form. However, it isn't the type of information that includes actual mentorship.

It took me several years from the time I understood the concept of "Smart Money" to learn what I needed to learn to start acting like it. Only after five years of working at it did smart investors start treating me like one.

When I finally had access to quality deals, I couldn't wait to call my player friends to show them these opportunities. They had all been in the same boat as me. We had all made good money and were trying to "do the right thing" with it. So I started calling my friends to explain this great deal that I had for them as an investment opportunity. I had all of my details down. I would explain the path I took to meeting these top investors and operators. I had all of the real estate knowledge to explain how the deal would work and all of the specific details anyone would want.

I would talk about safety first, and then discuss the return and the upside only after they were convinced I was covering the downside - that I was protecting them and their money. I had practiced my presentation and anticipated all of the questions I thought were important to a serious investor. I would show the players I called that I was different. I had it all laid out. It was a no-brainer to invest with me. I had the team, the safety, and the return. I had the answer. I was very confident and started making my calls.

Since these were friends, I felt I would get a very positive response. The first guy I called was happy to hear from me. We had a great

Fast Broke

conversation catching up on life stuff. Then I started with my presentation. I was enthusiastic. After all, I was doing my friends a big favor. Here I was giving them the keys to the vault. We never had the opportunity to invest with people of this quality as players. I was handing them the fruits of my years of work in figuring out the system. What a huge deal for them.

But soon I noticed a strange thing happening. On the other end of the phone, I could hear the attention drifting. I reached out to make sure that they were getting it. But the more I explained this great opportunity, the farther away the conversation went. I didn't know what was happening. How could this be misunderstood? Where is the jumping for joy I expected? I was being tuned out. I was at a loss to explain it. I had all of these hopes, and then my friend delivered the death knell.

"I'll have my guy look at it."

How can you tell the difference between a good "look at it" and a bad "look at it"? First, there was a total lack of enthusiasm in the answer. Most players have guys whose job is to say "No." Players get pitched all the time and often have a mechanism of getting out of uncomfortable situations, whether it's a rabid fan or an unwanted investment deal. "But what if the guy likes it?" you ask. He won't like it because he doesn't make any money off it. I didn't offer it to him to repackage, take a large cut, and then offer it to my friend. So he has no reason to like it.

I tried a different path to see if I could get my friend to look at this opportunity as *an investor*, not as a guy getting pitched. I asked if he had any questions to engage him and only got a polite "No thanks, I'm good." Of course I could tell my presentation was received like a turd in the punchbowl.

After a series of these experiences, I started to get it.

"Dumb Money" doesn't have enough investment knowledge to know a good deal from a bad deal. "Dumb Money" closes the door and leaves it up to "their guy" to handle the investment decisions.

I had another group of friends that were professional investors. These were not athletes. They were people from different walks of life who have taken the sport of investing as a full-time job. They read, go to seminars, join mastermind groups, look at deals, ask tons of questions and mentor each other. We all took an interest in helping each other learn and gain access to things. When one of us came across a deal that interested us, we would share it with the group for discussion and dissection. It was a great exercise that doubled as a tremendous learning experience.

The biggest difference was the total level of enthusiasm that I received. The group was eager to look at a deal and examine it. We all realized that very few deals were taken all the way to investment, but each deal provided a new lesson. The other element of the discussions was this group of friends was looking for good investments. Those in the group felt confident that they would know one when they saw it. When the right one came along, we would discuss it with vigor. Then when all of the examinations were done, the next question I would hear was, "How much can I get?"

The difference in each experience was like night and day. The energy was great, the investors were eager and the questions were enthusiastic. The process took a fraction of the time and was without the frustration of talking to people who didn't "get it." It was a true

Fast Broke

win-win. The investor was able to access deals he really wanted and was actively seeking. I got the satisfaction of sharing an opportunity I believed in enough to invest in myself. I also received the same treatment in return. When a friend came across a deal he liked, I would get a call to look at it and have the chance to participate as well. That's because another difference between "Smart Money" and "Dumb Money" is that "Smart Money" brings additional value to the entire process. It may be expertise, other investors or access to other opportunities. If nothing else, "Smart Money" becomes a person to bounce ideas off, get an outside opinion from and help generate ideas.

As I continued to repeat the process, a few things became clear. I was continually trying to help friends who were not experienced investors. I thought I could bring them great value by teaching them how to invest while they were seeing and investing in terrific opportunities. They could gain access to top-level people with a track record of success who could help secure their investment futures. Most important, I could be a catalyst in "teaching them to fish" by sharing the benefit of my experiences, which allowed them to avoid the long and difficult process of trial and error that I went through.

After a while, I learned another feature of "Dumb Money": *They don't want to get it.* Why learn it yourself when you can pawn off the work on somebody else? I became very frustrated as I felt I was not doing a good job of teaching my fellow players what I had learned. I finally got that it was not about information at all. It wasn't about what someone knew; it was about his attitude. "Smart Money" wants to learn and develop. It wants to add value. And most importantly, *it wants to grow.* "Dumb Money," on the other hand, is fine being dumb. It doesn't have a real interest in learning, growing or adding value. Don't get me wrong. "Dumb Money" wants to make more money. It just doesn't want to do the things it takes to make getting rich a likely outcome.

Raising Easy Capital

What I discovered rather quickly was that calling people who had money but no financial education was a slow, difficult and frustrating process. It involved a lot of work and hand-holding. I would lay out a terrific opportunity, only to get a blank stare in return. Or I would be instructed to call "their guy."

However, the opposite was true when I called a qualified investor. When I spoke to someone who was passionate about investing and had taken the time to really learn about it, it was easy to put something together. It didn't take very long to figure out that my time was best spent calling only savvy investors, those known as "Smart Money." Why would I spend hours calling people with money but without financial sophistication, only to get poor results? My time is also very valuable, and when I was busy with a quality deal, trying convince unmotivated investors was a tremendous waste of time, especially when it was so simple to share a good deal with a motivated investor who was looking for a good deal. This was an "Ah-ha" moment. When I finally figured this out, I found that raising capital was a pleasure.

I became much more efficient, and as an added bonus I discovered that raising capital was a sharing experience rather than a selling experience. I was dealing with like-minded people who were looking for the very thing that I was offering. I was investing in any deal I presented, and it was a pleasure to spend time with passionate investors. I also found I would learn more about investing when I engaged experienced people in an investment conversation. They would invariably ask me questions on topics I had never considered. It

Fast Broke

was a true win-win experience! I used this lesson to raise several million dollars of investment capital with ease. And over time, it just got easier.

Nothing makes an opportunity call go more smoothly than calling someone for whom you have already made money. When I called with another deal that is as good or better, it became a lock that they would give it a hard look. It was easy for me to see that success breeds success. When a good deal meets a good investor, magic happens. And once you make someone money, they are always answering your calls.

I also quickly realized that the opposite must be true. If a promoter had a deal that didn't have a high chance of success or was naturally risky, he would definitely look for someone who did not have the same level of experience. As you know, in many situations you don't have a clue whether it will work or not. You may be opening a specialty store and don't know if your product will sell. You might want to open a restaurant or a bar, two businesses which have a punishing failure rate. Or you might be developing in an unproven area where you might do everything right, but the market simply doesn't materialize.

In these cases, the capital raiser must find someone whose "pencil isn't that sharp." This is where inexperience as an investor really pays off - for the salesperson, that is. Don't forget that every deal is a good one ... for somebody. There are plenty of deals that make money for the promoter and everyone else gets burned. The bad part of this strategy is that there is little repeat business.

The way to lure an investor into a risky deal is to emphasize the benefits of the deal that aren't about making money. Bars and restaurants are the best for this.

Fast Broke

"Imagine being able to entertain all of your friends."

"Look how cool you name will look over the door."

"Wouldn't it be great to have your own hang-out spot where you own the private room in the back?"

"See how much money _____ is making?"

You get the idea. Remember that there are many benefits to certain investments that outweigh the money factor. There is prestige, fun (for any business thought of as a toy), or being high profile. It can generate money that goes into another business, such as when a manufacturer opens a store to sell and market its own products. Some businesses create content for others, such as when an actor produces movies in which he also stars.

Many people start a business to give themselves or someone else a job. Many people with a professional skill create a business around it and open up a shop or business of some kind.

The key is to be able to understand the nature of the opportunity. Remember, someone with a bad deal that pays a high commission is always on the lookout for a guy with money and no financial savvy. He then can sell the sizzle, not the steak.

Should I show a bad deal to a smart investor?

As you see these two forces at work, it is easy to see that the opposite is always true as well. I learned not to take a good deal to an uneducated investor, as it is a waste of time and energy. I will only take a good deal to an experienced investor who will see that it is a moneymaker and wants to be part of it. It also stands to reason that

Fast Broke

you would not take a bad deal to a good investor. Why take a deal to someone who will see it as something toxic?

First of all, you will ruin your chance to get in with a good investor who may otherwise invest with you at another time. Second of all, you will soon develop the reputation as someone not to be trusted. Most importantly - as if those reasons aren't important enough - successful people often will burn someone they perceive to be trying to rip them off. It is easy to see entire investment groups cut off to you by trying to pass off junk. In today's world of networking and the Internet, it is easier than ever to spread the word far and wide to avoid doing business with someone.

Once I truly understood this concept, I saw why most athletes invest poorly. *They don't deserve to see great deals.*

This one mechanism is the single biggest reason most people fail financially, while only a few succeed. I have spoken to many highly successful money managers who won't manage athletes for this very reason.

Fast Broke

Fast Broke

Chapter 3

Starting Out

When I was nearing the end of my college career, it was becoming clear that I was going to be a first-round pick in the NBA draft. For several reasons, the draft was much different in the 1980s. The salaries were lower, social media did not exist and television coverage was minimal.

Still, it was a big deal. I remember hearing that the Utah Jazz had drafted me with the 13th overall pick. I was kind of shocked. I didn't know much about the team or the city. I had not spoken to any team officials before the draft. The fans were kind of shocked as well, as I remember being heartily booed by Jazz fans back in Salt Lake City. They wanted the team to pick a different guy. So it was not a very auspicious beginning.

After I signed my first contract, I was an instant millionaire! My contract was for five years at just over $200,000 per year. Considering I had only $647 to my name, I sure felt rich.

I grew up middle class in an all-white suburb of Syracuse, New York. My father was one of the greatest basketball players of his era, so I grew up in the family business. He had a long career as one of the NBA's pioneer stars, having played 16 years. In those days, the money was minimal, so many players had to work in the summers to make ends meet. Few players had long careers because – believe it or not - once they got married and started a family, their salaries were too small to allow them to keep playing.

My father started buying and building small apartment houses to

Fast Broke

supplement his income and eventually made that his full-time business,

We were not poor but were never considered well off. I may be dating myself, but I used to joke that Richie Cunningham from the TV show "Happy Days" could have lived on my street.

Still, I had a fun childhood, had everything that I needed and much of what I wanted. I just didn't want very much. My parents grew up during the Great Depression and many of my attitudes about money were shaped by their experiences. We didn't talk much about money, and I had no real education about finance.

I was a smart kid, though, and graduated Syracuse with honors as a chemistry major. I was an Academic All-American, won postgraduate academic scholarships, and was one of only two students from Syracuse to be nominated for the prestigious Rhodes Scholarship.

The only reason I bring that up is that with all of that education and academic success, I still was totally unprepared to succeed financially once entering the NBA. Luckily, I didn't make enough money to totally screw things up. But looking back, I am amazed at what I didn't know.

I moved thousands of miles from home. I had never rented or bought a house, car or any other big-ticket item. I never had an investment account or did my taxes. I certainly never had a financial advisor or a retirement plan. And as I mentioned earlier, I didn't even own a washer and dryer.

How in the world was I expected to be thrown into the deep end of the financial pool and learn how to swim?

I started out doing what most athletes do: I asked my agent for advice.

Fast Broke

Chapter 3

Starting Out

When I was nearing the end of my college career, it was becoming clear that I was going to be a first-round pick in the NBA draft. For several reasons, the draft was much different in the 1980s. The salaries were lower, social media did not exist and television coverage was minimal.

Still, it was a big deal. I remember hearing that the Utah Jazz had drafted me with the 13th overall pick. I was kind of shocked. I didn't know much about the team or the city. I had not spoken to any team officials before the draft. The fans were kind of shocked as well, as I remember being heartily booed by Jazz fans back in Salt Lake City. They wanted the team to pick a different guy. So it was not a very auspicious beginning.

After I signed my first contract, I was an instant millionaire! My contract was for five years at just over $200,000 per year. Considering I had only $647 to my name, I sure felt rich.

I grew up middle class in an all-white suburb of Syracuse, New York. My father was one of the greatest basketball players of his era, so I grew up in the family business. He had a long career as one of the NBA's pioneer stars, having played 16 years. In those days, the money was minimal, so many players had to work in the summers to make ends meet. Few players had long careers because – believe it or not - once they got married and started a family, their salaries were too small to allow them to keep playing.

My father started buying and building small apartment houses to

Fast Broke

supplement his income and eventually made that his full-time business,

We were not poor but were never considered well off. I may be dating myself, but I used to joke that Richie Cunningham from the TV show "Happy Days" could have lived on my street.

Still, I had a fun childhood, had everything that I needed and much of what I wanted. I just didn't want very much. My parents grew up during the Great Depression and many of my attitudes about money were shaped by their experiences. We didn't talk much about money, and I had no real education about finance.

I was a smart kid, though, and graduated Syracuse with honors as a chemistry major. I was an Academic All-American, won postgraduate academic scholarships, and was one of only two students from Syracuse to be nominated for the prestigious Rhodes Scholarship.

The only reason I bring that up is that with all of that education and academic success, I still was totally unprepared to succeed financially once entering the NBA. Luckily, I didn't make enough money to totally screw things up. But looking back, I am amazed at what I didn't know.

I moved thousands of miles from home. I had never rented or bought a house, car or any other big-ticket item. I never had an investment account or did my taxes. I certainly never had a financial advisor or a retirement plan. And as I mentioned earlier, I didn't even own a washer and dryer.

How in the world was I expected to be thrown into the deep end of the financial pool and learn how to swim?

I started out doing what most athletes do: I asked my agent for advice.

Fast Broke

Typically, the team can recommend a realtor to help players find a house or apartment. It is usually a friend of the coach or general manager, so that process is a crapshoot.

Next you start to stumble around. You find a bank and open a checking account. You call American Express and apply for a credit card. Wow, I found out that I was actually credit worthy. I was a man now!

I remember the feeling of how difficult it was just getting simple things done. Who did I call to get my utilities turned on? What about cable TV and phone service? I didn't know that you had to sign up for trash service. I thought that it just happened. I wondered why my trashcan was always full when all of my neighbors had their cans emptied. I felt pretty dumb asking the neighbor about that one.

In my first year in the NBA, I learned many financial lessons. The first was the difference between gross income and net income. When my first paycheck came, I felt like I had been hit with a ton of bricks. Why was this check so much smaller than I was expecting? That was an eye opener, let me tell you.

Then I had to buy stuff. I moved out to Salt Lake City with whatever I could fit in my car. I had no furniture, TV, kitchen stuff or other basic necessities. I didn't get much investing done for two reasons: I didn't know much about it and I didn't have any money. After rent and buying stuff, there wasn't much left, even on an NBA salary.

After that season, however, I started putting away as much money as I could. I was a good saver and slowly built a small nest egg of cash. I started reading the financial magazines in an attempt to get as much information about investing as I could. Remember, this was pre-Internet, so access to information was limited. My agent was on the

Fast Broke

East Coast but I communicated with him as often as possible. He was busy with his business, though, so he wasn't very helpful.

Over the next few years, I found a stockbroker to buy and sell stocks, bought some life insurance and invested a small amount of money in income property and other investments. I didn't have a clue what I was doing, and it showed in my results. For some reason, my income property was always rented but never provided any income.

Once, I bought a wind turbine on one of those wind farms. How do you screw that up? The wind blows, and you make money, right? Well, it turns out that mine rusted out and stopped working after a year. I never did get a good explanation on that one. All I got was the tax deduction.

Then I got approached about a deal that was a tax-saving opportunity. The guy explained that his deal would lose all of the money that I put into it but would give me five dollars in tax deductions for every dollar lost. So if I "invested" $10,000 I would be entitled to $50,000 in tax deductions, saving me $25,000 in taxes. Was this a good deal?

I was learning by the age-old method of trial and error. But all I mastered was the error part. And I considered myself smart, with a college education.

By the end of my seventh NBA season, I had finally figured out some things. I had hired a good accountant who understood small business and entrepreneurship (although it wasn't called that at the time). I had a decent stockbroker and was a really good saver. I wasn't making a killing, but at least I hadn't blown everything.

Soon, however, things were going to change. Free agency just became common and I was about to hit it big - relatively speaking, that is.

Chapter 4

Learning the Basics

Looking for Love in all the Wrong Places

I signed my biggest contract, which averaged about $1.5 million per year over seven years. At one point I said, "This is it. I want to be set when I'm done playing." So I met with my agent, and we sat down with the investment guys and put together a plan. I looked at all the projections that showed if I did my part and saved, at the end of my career I would have plenty of money to live a very nice lifestyle. My investments would generate more than enough income that I needed.

From then on, I received monthly reports showing the progress of my investments. The first page always said "Congratulations! You've met or exceeded your saving goal for this month!" It was nice to have that knowledge every month. Just like working out every day, I was putting in the energy and the effort to make sure that I did my part and gave them the resources with which to work.

But soon I started noticing some funny things. For instance, the stock market was skyrocketing, but my portfolio didn't seem to change much. If anything, it just kind of languished. It turned out that value stocks paid more commissions than growth stocks, but value stocks didn't budge during that time. It was only the growth stocks. I missed out on that completely.

There was no exposure to income real estate or dividend-paying stocks, the things that generate income in retirement. Also, there was a lot of emphasis on cash value life insurance, which I found out is the highest commission product out there.

Fast Broke

Here I was working hard, playing ball, putting money away, deferring the purchases one would typically would make, only to find out over the years that nothing really was happening. Outside of my own commitment to saving money, I wasn't getting any boost from my investments. I knew on some level this didn't seem to be a successful plan, but I didn't know what else there was. I didn't have access to truly wealthy people to understand how they invested. I didn't have access to better business deals that were safe and paid a good return, whether it was income property or commercial real estate.

Much later I would realize one of the traps that snare many people. It's one of the ways that the game is rigged for you to fail. Typically the deals that pay you - the investor - the least also pay the commission salesman the most. That how they get sold. Otherwise no one would ever look at them.

I had the luxury of having a long window where I could live off my salary and still have plenty left over. I didn't need to dip into the investments. I had to do all the right things now, defer that gratification until after I was done playing, and then I could live the way I want to the rest of my life.

As far as I was concerned, from all the financial magazines and other education that I studied religiously, I was doing the right things. But what I also found was that the mistake I was making was that the fees were so high that no matter what the investments returned, I could never gain financial traction. It was like trying to run 10 miles per hour in the face of a 50 mph headwind. You can't move forward that way.

When I finally became financially literate, I realized the information I was getting by reading the major money periodicals were being written by the very people profiting from this charade. The world of

Fast Broke

institutional investing, banks, mutual funds, insurance companies and others is essentially a large marketing machine designed to separate you from your money. You work hard. You give it to them. They take most of it, give you back a little, and that's investing. At least, that's what they tell you.

Again, the line that every athlete hears from his advisor is "It's hard to play ball. You play ball, let me handle this part." So you're encouraged not to look at it or learn about it. Your advisors know that if you really knew what you were doing, you would cut out 90 percent of the people in your life, including them. You wouldn't hire the people you hire. You wouldn't support the people you support. You wouldn't buy many of the things you do. You wouldn't invest in the things that you do. Remember, the machine is designed for you to be separated from your money, on every level.

What had been most frustrating for me was that I knew when I started my career I looked at this as the one opportunity I had to make a lot of money. I wanted to make sure that when I was done playing, I would be set for life. So I spent a lot of time and attention doing my part. I hired who I thought were good quality advisors. I started with my agent, who was my contract negotiator. He was the best in the industry. He was credited for creating basketball's agent business back in the 1960s, was a terrific contract negotiator, and, frankly, a family friend. He was a contemporary of my dad, so he was kind of like a second dad. I was the same age as his kids, and we got to be very close. We used to spend time together in the summer and do a lot of the family thing. He negotiated some terrific contracts.

I also had an advisor who also was an agent. I didn't use him as an agent, but more as an oversight manager. He was a Harvard attorney, a fraternity brother at Syracuse and a well-respected guy. I also had a

Fast Broke

stockbroker who was a vice president at one of the major firms.

I was doing all the "right" things. I was not a frivolous spender. I put an investment plan in place and followed it religiously. I saved my money to enjoy later. The money was there. It wasn't embezzled in any way but it just wasn't growing the way I thought it could or should.

The investments, if you want to call them that, were essentially traditional mutual funds and some stock positions, a few small percentages in individual real estate rentals, a condo here or a rental house there. These never seemed to generate much income, but I didn't really know any better. I thought I was doing the right things by being a saver.

I was always told that it was very complicated. You need a professional. You need someone to do it for you. And I was encouraged not to learn, although I learned from the resources I had at the time - the top money magazines and investing shows on TV, which were few. I was conscientious about tracking expenses to maximize tax deductions and all the things that you're supposed to do.

Early in my career, I had not signed big contracts. In the early 1980s, I was making $200,000 to $250,000 annually, which drops to slightly more than $100,000 after taxes. It wasn't "get rich" money, but it was "start with a nest egg" money, where you could put away $20,000-$50,000 each year if you were a very good saver.

In the middle of my career I signed what at the time was a huge contract averaging almost $1.5 million per year. Again, by the time you remove taxes, agent fees, and all the other things they ding you with, I took home between $700,000 and $800,000 a year. By living conservatively, I was able to save over half of my net income, which

Fast Broke

was my goal.

As time went along, on some level I knew this didn't seem to be getting me rich. I couldn't imagine that really successful people did this, but I had no access to knowing what they actually did. I didn't understand generating passive income streams, developing a business or investing in one, or how to meet the right people. I just kept doing my thing, storing money away. When I married Wendy, she saw right away that something was wrong.

It just didn't smell right, and when we looked into it we found that the investment advisory was charging me a fee to manage the money, while collecting large fees on the investment products. Essentially what they were doing was double dipping, and instead of putting me in products that were great investments, they would put me in products that paid high commissions. Obviously, if you have to pay a high commission it's not a very good product. I dug into it more, and there were several glaring examples of things that just didn't pass the smell test.

I had a friend of mine who was a very successful businessman look over my history. The first thing he said was if your agent is charging you a percentage of your gross salary, he is overcharging you. It was the first time I really understood. He said a top money manager would only charge you a small percentage, perhaps 1 percent to 2 percent of the money that he manages, not your gross income. My manager was charging me 5 percent of my *gross* income. Essentially, if you do the math, if I was being charged 5 percent of my gross income, which was roughly 10 percent of my net income. When you look at the money that I actually have under investments, probably half again of that, I was paying between 20 percent and 25 percent commission every year on my investments.

And that's just the fee that I saw. Remember, he was also collecting fees on the investment products, plus collecting other bonuses from placing my money. It's hard to get ahead when you are being charged over 40 percent in fees on investments that return between 5 percent and 10 percent each year.

Again, those are the types of things the investment world doesn't want you to get. Of course, I didn't understand that until later. My friend explained, "How can he earn you enough money to justify you having him there? If you did nothing, you would make 40 percent more than you're making now."

So I finally woke up to that. Wendy saw it right away. Because she didn't know the guy, she wasn't caught up in being blinded by family loyalty. She could see right away that something wasn't right. I ended up calling him on it, and his response was that his fee was the standard of the industry. He just forgot to mention which industry he meant.

At this point, I had two years left on my contract and told him, "This isn't right, how it's going. I think a good settlement would be to waive the last two years of the future commissions due on my existing player contract, and we'll call it even. It won't cost you anything since it's money that you never had." It was a much lower amount than the investment commissions he overcharged me for, but I didn't want to get into a lawsuit over it. He said, "Absolutely not. You're going to pay me every penny." I was forced to sue him, and I did, successfully.

Once we dug into his finances, we found out that the way he and his partners were investing was double- and sometimes triple-dipping. They not only got a sales commission but also a percentage of a deal for putting me in it, on top of me paying them a commission to do it. The only good news was that they didn't embezzle money. They just overcharged fees. Sometimes you have to look really hard to find good news.

What really happened was that as time went on and the agency got more successful, the relationship changed. They set up the business thinking we worked for them, not them for us.

That relationship very much changed, and one of the points the agent made was that he had never been sued, and how dare I be the first. He had an impeccable reputation. The reality was very different. One day when my lawyer had his assistant run down and file the lawsuit, the clerk at the court asked, "Are you representing all the people suing this guy?"

It turned out there were at least a dozen active lawsuits. He just settled and had confidentiality agreements, so nobody knew. The punch line was in the middle of our lawsuit, he ended up passing away on a boat with his mistress, after a lifetime of preaching family values.

The frustrating part was that I did everything I thought was right, everything I was told and taught was right, only to find out that everyone got the anticipated results – except me. That's the way the institutional system is set up. It is designed for you to get a little – and for them to get a lot. They want you to get just enough so you don't wake up, figure out that it's not that hard and do it yourself. And remember that all the information you get on investing comes from the guy selling you the deal, whether it's the bank or brokerage house or insurance company. The ones giving you the information are the ones who have the vested interest in you doing it.

It was a very aggravating experience, because all those years I was doing the right thing. It was like being on a diet and exercising only to

Fast Broke

find out that you were eating all the wrong foods because you were told they were the right foods. Ten years go by, and you didn't lose a pound. That's what I felt like with all that effort.

Fast Broke

Chapter 5

Left Foot First

Let me give you an example of how easy it is to get in trouble by not having a strong financial education.

My wife Wendy is a springboard diver. She won an NCAA championship, nine national championships, and competed in the 1988 Summer Olympics in Seoul, South Korea. In 2004 we were at the Olympic Diving trials, and one of the young divers was talking to Wendy, trying to get some advice. She asked, "When you're on the board and it's a key dive, and you're nervous, what do you think about to calm yourself down?" Wendy looked at her and said, "Left foot first." The girl was like, "What? Left foot first? That's it?"

Wendy was explaining to the girl that what happens when you get really nervous is you are in your head thinking, instead of your body doing your motion. By taking your left foot first, it keys into everything that you know how to do. Once you start on the correct path, then your training takes over and everything falls into place. If you end up stepping wrong out of the box, there's no fixing it.

For me, this metaphor was very impactful. It describes how easy it is to execute a plan when you start on the right path and stay on it. But if you get off the path or start in the wrong direction, there's no fixing it. It's very, very hard to get back on track if you make early wrong decisions.

So the key is to spend the time going in the right direction first. As you make adjustments along the way, at least you're adjusting to the right direction. If you start with your right foot first, then there's no way to get your feet back together and do anything successfully. That's what "left foot first" means.

It's amazing how many of us who work very hard to get something, myself included, find out that in the end you never really wanted it in the first place.

Let me give you an example.

I was talking to a player who played in the 1980s and 1990s and had the good fortune of signing a huge contract at the time, $40 million over five years. He reasoned that he would dedicate one year of his contract toward building his dream home, so he built an $8 million house. Sounds reasonable, right? He still had the bulk of his earnings left for the rest of his life.

But did he accomplish what he set out to do? Actually, no. Let's look at the mistakes he made in his presumptions and you will see that he did not put his "left foot first." As a matter of fact, he was so far off track that even if he did everything right, by starting off in the wrong direction there was no fixing it.

The player's first problem was that he forgot about his biggest partner, the IRS. Remember that his $8 million annual gross salary is about $4 million net. So he actually committed not one but two full years of salary to building his house.

Problem #2 was that he now had an $8 million empty house. To fill up such a large home requires another huge outlay of money. The house was 25,000 square feet with several acres of grounds and pools. Typically, it takes about 50 percent of the value of a home to completely outfit it, no matter the size. It needs furniture, artwork, window coverings and decorations. The garage needs some cars.

Fast Broke

There are clothes, appliances, TVs and audio equipment to buy. And don't forget the pool furnishings and big boy toys. There is probably a jet ski or two, a fishing boat, golf cart, etc. Plus there will be personal items like jewelry and other items.

So now he has used a third year of his contract in furnishing the house.

Problem #3 is maintenance. The property taxes and insurance will run 3 percent of the value of the home every year. Add in utilities, repairs, lawn care, pool care, cleaning and other fixed costs and you have a large revolving expense. If you want to cover these costs in perpetuity, you need to set aside a fund that earns enough money to pay it. If it costs 5 percent of the value of the home to run and maintain it (a standard number, regardless of the size of the home), then you need to set aside the value of the home in cash and earn 5 percent on that money.

The player intended to commit one year worth of earnings toward his dream home, but by not putting his "left foot first" he actually committed a full four years of a five-year contract into the house. You can easily see that once he stepped in the wrong direction, there was no fixing it no matter how well he executed his plan.

So how big a house could the player really afford if he followed his own rule? If you work the math backwards, he can "only" afford a house with the total purchase price of $1.6 million. Surprised? I thought you would be. While a house with a value of $1.6 million is hardly a shack, it seems like with a guaranteed contract of $40 million a player could safely afford more. After all, if he went to the bank and asked for a loan, he could qualify to purchase a $20 million home!

With that kind of buying power, is it any surprise that the realtor is

Fast Broke

only showing him homes for $8 million and up? Can you see how his wife, family and friends would encourage that? Remember, everybody benefits if the player buys the huge mansion. The commissions are larger, the house is nicer and the player gets what he feels that he deserves.

What about you and your situation?

- Do you think that your realtor and your banker or mortgage broker encourage you to get as much house as you can qualify for?
- Do they explain how your earnings will continue to grow so you can afford it?
- Do you underestimate remodel and decorating costs?
- Do you splurge on furniture or the home theatre because it's your home?
- Did you not realize that the property taxes were set when the house was worth less, and are surprised that they double the first year that you own the home?

While we make fun of the athlete that buys ridiculous mansions, those same forces that cause him to overspend are at work in your life. That's why we look at the athlete as the examples, but you need to remember to look at what's happening in your life.

Fast Broke

Chapter 6

It's In No One's Interest That You Get It!

All players entering the NBA participate in the Rookie Transition Program. The league and the players association require every new player to attend a weeklong training session before the season starts. The program is an intense immersion type experience designed to open player's eyes to NBA life.

All kinds of lifestyle topics are covered. They cover wealth and investing. They cover health. They cover sex education, drug education and other topics players need to be aware of before entering this crazy universe of pro sports. It was held in Orlando where I was playing at the time, so I was invited by the Players Association to come in as a "coach" for one of the groups of incoming rookies.

My group had 15 young players who had been drafted or were going to a team's training camp. There were almost 100 players in all. I would attend the seminar lectures with the players, manage their educational materials, and at the end of the event open up some time for Q&A to make sure that they got all of their questions answered. What did they want to know that either wasn't addressed or confused them?

The players had to absorb a tremendous amount of specific information in a short period of time. As the young guys started asking questions it became obvious there were some basic big picture issues that they hadn't picked up.

I started having some realizations. I asked my group to do an exercise: Write down all the people you are going to have any kind of a financial transaction with in your pro life. We started on the white board. We picked out about 30 different people. You had the car salesman and the realtor. You had your agent and your family. You had the jeweler. You had your buddies. You had the life insurance guy. You had the stockbroker. You even had baby mamas, although they weren't called that back at the time.

This list went on and on, and we grouped them into three categories:

1) People trying to sell you stuff: the car guy, the suit guy, the jeweler, etc.
2) The advisors: The accountant, the realtor, the insurance agent, the stockbroker, etc.
3) The people you support: your family, your friends, etc.

We started by saying, "Let's see how many people on this list are incentivized by you having more money after you've dealt with them than when you started." In other words, how many guys get paid by you making money rather than spending money?

We just started at the top. Car guy? No. Tailor? No. Jeweler? Hell no. We quickly crossed all of those people off the list. It was immediately obvious that they wanted to sell you as much as they could without regard to what you actually needed.

Next up were the "advisors." What about your agent? He cares for you, right? Maybe, but remember once you're done playing ball, he's done representing you. He doesn't make any more money. His game is simple. The union has capped his fees for negotiating your contract at 4 percent of the gross salary. The day you sign the deal, you owe him that for the entire life of the contract. He doesn't ever need to speak to you again.

Fast Broke

But he knows that you want him to do all kinds of things for you. So he sets up a service division. He wants to provide as many services you will pay for while you are an active player. He can charge extra fees for bill paying, tax preparation, house hunting, offseason travel arrangements, car purchases and anything else that you will pay him to do.

The vast majority of these things you can do yourself, but he will try to convince you that you should just worry about basketball and leave the rest to him. Plus, investing is too complicated, so he will handle that for you as well. Imagine the fee stream that's possible in this deal.

What about your real estate agent? After all, your house is your biggest asset, right? Let's think about that. Their commission is determined by how much house you buy, so they want you to buy as big a house as you can qualify for – not one that is a sensible fit for you and your family. Maybe a $1 million house is best for you financially, but you can qualify for a $4 million house. They want you to buy the $4 million house, even though you could go broke keeping up with the payments. And what if you get traded in two years? They get to sell it again. So they're not on your side.

We continued down the list. We even discussed people who you think would want to make money for you. What about your stockbroker or insurance agent? Do you pay them on commission or performance? Virtually all stockbrokers get paid on commission, because stockbrokers on that level know that you don't know what you're doing. So they just churn your account. That way they can pretend they are actively investing your money. Insurance products pay massive commissions. Do you think they explain that as accredited investors you can buy the exact same products with *no commission*? Have you ever heard of *private placement life insurance*? I doubt it.

The reality is that top quality advisors don't want "dumb money" because it's too much work. The good ones get plenty of business and don't want the headaches that come with working with unsophisticated clients. Why bother? The scam artists know what lies to tell to get your business. They usually chase the good ones away.

What about your family? They want you to save money, right? Do they? What if by learning what you should really do, you figure out that you wouldn't be supporting all these people, or to the level that you do? They don't want you to know better than that. They want you to give them all your money, so they didn't count.

I was counseling one player who made big money before going broke. He said to me the most dangerous thing I ever heard. He told me that he loved his mother so much he would give her his last dime. I thought about that and asked, "Do you really hate her that much?" He was shocked when I explained how painful it would be for her to raise you from poverty to financial freedom, only to lose it all and return to poverty. If you spent half of what you do on her now, she could live well forever. She had guilted him into giving her all of what the super wealthy player moms got. Only he couldn't sustain it and finally did give her his last dime. I bet that didn't feel very good after all.

We ultimately figured out that there isn't one person on the list who is motivated by a player being successful. They are motivated only by a player giving them some of their money. That was probably the biggest eye-opener for young players. Just doing that exercise made me realize how rigged the system truly is.

During that Rookie Transition Program, two future star players were there who had vastly different post-career paths. One clearly didn't get it and one certainly did. I remember sitting in one of the sessions

Fast Broke

where the topic was league security and the discussion was centered on some of the ways players can get into trouble. The league security officer asked the entire group who had already bought a car. About a quarter of the hands went up, which was curious as few, if any, of the players had gotten paid yet.

One of the players was Allen Iverson. He had no use for this event and sat leaning back with his arms folded wearing a major scowl on his face. The only reason he showed up at all was that attendance is mandatory to enter the league. When he was called on, he shared that he had bought a Mercedes 600. Then he was asked if he had any issues being a 20-year-old young black man in a sweat suit, wearing gold chains and driving a $100,000 car. He shared that he had been pulled over several times and questioned, especially in white neighborhoods. He was then asked if he felt he was being hassled. His reply clearly showed that he didn't get it: He said he was hassled when they found his gun!

Fast forward 15 years and it seems clear that Iverson never got it. He was involved in several lawsuits claiming he was not paying his bills amid reports that he had blown through over $200 million and was broke. Dumb money.

The other player was Ray Allen. He was in my group and was totally engaged in the program for the entire week. He paid attention, asked lots of questions and got a lot out of the experience. I remember one conversation we had about life on the road. I joked with him that at some time during the season, after being in five different hotels in an eight-day stretch, he will get into the elevator, stick out his finger to push the button for his floor and have no idea what his room number was. I told him that he would have to go to the front desk and ask them what room he was in. Ray laughed and said that would never happen to him.

We ended up playing against each other about 10 games into the season. During warmups, he ran over to me and blurted out, "I didn't even make it through training camp." He told me all about standing in the elevator with his finger pointing at the buttons, laughing his ass off as he remembered our conversation. He couldn't wait to tell me about it.

Midway through his career, Ray was offered a "max contract." It was a predetermined amount that was the most money he could receive under the league guidelines and as such didn't need to be negotiated. It is typical for a player to use an agent to negotiate contracts for a predetermined fee of 4 percent of the gross salary for the life of the contract. For a long-term contract, the fee can run in the millions for a couple of hours of work. But Ray had learned some things and took his financial health seriously. He smartly determined that a max deal didn't need any negotiating, since the terms were already set. So he figured all he needed was an attorney to review the contract for a few hours of billable time, instead of seven years of huge payments for an unnecessary job. Pretty sharp. Smart Money.

It's not just athletes; it's everyplace you go. Probably 95 percent of advisors - and I use that term loosely - are incentivized by doing business, not making you money. They don't have to be good to get paid. They don't have to make you money to get paid.

Successful people know they would rather pay a guy 20 percent of the profits than a commission, even though it may be three times the money. That's a better deal for them. Guys on a profit share are motivated to make you money, not just to make transactions happen. Even though I was sharing that exercise, it was a huge discovery and it

Fast Broke

really cleared up a lot of things for me.

When you see how super wealthy, unsophisticated young men are completely surrounded by a machine designed to do nothing but separate them from their money, it's easy to see why so many players fail. Now look at your group you have around you. Is it any different?

Fast Broke

Chapter 7

My Awakening

Around the time when I was retiring, I was taking a lot of personal development courses with a company called Landmark Education. I was doing a lot of personal growth and finally understanding a lot of emotional things that were in my own way of greater success. In the middle of building our dream house, Wendy and I were sitting down watching TV one day, and Robert Kiyosaki, the author of the *Rich Dad* series of books, had his first big event on "The Oprah Winfrey Show." He was talking about things like financial literacy, developing income streams and replacing your job's income. He touched on asset protection and safety, understanding business and how to generate from nothing.

He was touching on all the subjects I had been looking for but couldn't put into words. In just that one hour, I had a huge awakening because Kiyosaki helped me understand what I was missing. I really needed to pursue the entrepreneur path, understand how to generate income and learn how to manage what I had. I had to open up to the world of abundance and learn how to generate rather than consume. It was a huge life-changing event. At the end of the show, he talked about how most people go broke when they start building their dream house – which we had just started doing. It was enlightening, but also aggravating.

Where were you five years ago?

For the first time, I started to understand what I was missing. I was also learning that what I was being fed was not very effective. It was like somebody opened the door to the path that I needed to be on. I had

Fast Broke

been constantly looking in all the wrong places, so the answers I needed were never there. Once I understood that I needed to look at the entrepreneur path, things start making sense. That was when my financial education really began in earnest.

What I really needed to understand was entrepreneurship. I needed to understand building income streams and how to generate business, because my only other solution was to generate income from my existing savings. It is very difficult to generate enough living income from interest without massive sums of money. I had a lot of money in the bank based on my earnings, but since I didn't play in the huge money era, it was not enough to generate the kind of interest income I needed. When I retired, I realized pretty quickly that I didn't really have a clue, even though I was a smart guy. I didn't have the knowledge to do what I needed to do.

So Wendy and I started by pursuing seminar education. We took seminars on all kinds of different areas: personal development, asset protection, stock trading, real estate investing, entity structures and others. I didn't know what I wanted to do nor did I know what I was good at. I knew that I had to learn before I acted, otherwise I would just set myself up for failure.

At the time I was a full-time TV analyst for the Seattle SuperSonics, so I was traveling regularly anyway. Wendy and I would just connect through different cities and take seminars that interested us. Sometimes we would go to one that would have previews of other events that interested us. We probably did three seminars a month for two years. We spent all the money I saved on college and ended up with our real life education. I had a great education in chemistry, but none in how to make money. That's how we got started, because I realized I had to learn the specialty knowledge that I lacked.

Fast Broke

As a brief aside, I made much more money using my financial education than I spent on it. Education was the best investment I ever made.

After watching that Oprah Winfrey show, I actually sat down and wrote Robert Kiyosaki a long letter introducing myself and emailed it to his office. I talked about how athletes really need to understand this message, and that I would love to meet him and discuss some of our issues. Over the next few weeks, I didn't hear back from him but saw on his website that he was doing an event in Los Angeles. We were in Orlando but knew people in Los Angeles and loved going there, so I took Wendy on a little "vacation." We went to his event at a hotel, which was a one night, three-hour preview.

We got there early, and before the event started I saw him walk by so I ran over to say hello. He was just about to go into a meeting with his then real estate advisor, Dolf De Roos. I just kind of barged in and introduced myself. He was not a sports guy, did not follow basketball and didn't know who I was. But he looked up and said, "You're the guy who sent me that email." Because I had sent him the email and took that action, he knew who I was and had a familiarity with my story. We talked for 15 minutes before he invited me to come back at the mid-event break and meet his wife, Kim, which we did.

After Wendy and I spent some time with Robert, he said, "Why don't you come up on stage, and we'll talk about athletes and why they struggle?" Ten minutes after he started the second half of the event, he brought me up on stage as if we were old friends. We had this great conversation about why athletes struggle with the way they invest and retire. Just the action of talking about it got me to understand it more and more. That was really the beginning of me finally getting it, going down the path of what I needed to know, and starting from zero. While

Fast Broke

I had a classical education and understood math and science, I did not understand the vagaries of investing, the different markets and finance.

After meeting with Robert at the first event, we went to his three-day event. He was holding an event in Dallas, right after his LA event. He said, "Why don't you guys come as my guests?" On the way home, we stopped in Dallas for his three-day event, which was on general financial literacy. I knew that this was the message I had been looking for. In Dallas, he had previews for some other guys selling their courses, and so that's how we started our quest. We met seminar guys at other events, or we talked to people we met at the event, and they recommended this guy or that guy.

We tracked them down, took their courses, and luckily we had the wherewithal to travel. Many of the events were held in Orlando or nearby in Atlanta and Tampa, which were all big seminar cities. We took a lot of events locally or in Las Vegas. We took a lot of different courses on virtually every topic. It was important to us that we had a thorough education.

We did every type of real estate: commercial, residential, multi-family. We studied buying and selling notes. We talked about tax liens and stock trading, whether it was buying and selling shares, options or currencies. We needed to understand the different strategies within those categories. We took general strategy courses, asset protection, business development, trusts, estate planning and tax entities – all kinds of different courses in everything that interested us. It was quite the education. Some of the courses were powerful. Some also sucked, but we always got something positive out of them.

The seminars all had home study courses as follow-ups. At one point

Fast Broke

my home library looked like a videotape and audiotape store.

We realized we had to start small and were eager to try out the techniques we were learning. I still had my employee job for a while, so I didn't give it up completely. I did my TV work and some other appearances. Wendy was the one really saying, "We've got to get out and do this." So we started.

We had a rule that for every course we took, we had to do something. We had to at least try it. How else would we know if we liked it or not? We flipped some small houses and did some paper trading in the stock market, for instance. We now had a great resource to set up an asset protection strategy, plan our tax strategy and find good investing advisors. We also met a lot of like-minded people along the way that we kept in contact with as a support group. After all, nothing is more terrifying than putting money on the line in an endeavor for the first time.

But I had some good pieces in place for success. I had studied and mastered my topic. I had a well thought-out strategy. I had a team in place to help me manage my business. I had a good coach. And most of all, I had the attitude that I would see it through and was committed to my success.

I spent my playing career being "Dumb Money" but was making the transition to being "Smart Money." This is the single most important key to financial success. I was earning the right to succeed.

Fast Broke

Chapter 8

How to Go Broke On $100 Million

We have all heard about the alarming statistics indicating that most professional athletes will be broke within five to seven years of retirement. And we all ask the same questions.

"How can this happen when they make all that money?"

"Who is advising these guys?"

"Where is their agent?"

"Why doesn't the league do something?"

Plus we have all heard the stories about the extravagant spending, the children out of wedlock, the bad investments and wonder, "How dumb can these guys be?"

The answer is much simpler than you think. And while we vicariously enjoy hearing the stories of the wild nightclub parties, the garages with six luxury cars and the necklaces with enough jewels to be seen from space, it is a myth that the sole reason players go broke is because they spend themselves to death. It certainly happens to some guys who spend themselves into the poor house, but they are the exception, not the rule. That is *not* the root cause of the problem. It is merely one of the symptoms.

You need to remember that many players come from poor backgrounds. Earlier, we discussed what typically happens when a person from a poor upbringing suddenly gets a huge windfall of cash. We also discussed how the system is designed to separate a player from his money while he is in many ways defenseless to stop it. We analyzed the difference between "Smart Money" and "Dumb Money" and how that distinction affects the players' outcomes. But you can see how, with the proper intervention and training, many of the outlandish behaviors can be controlled. Will that solve the problem? Is it that easy to lower the player failure rate to near zero? Hardly.

It is time to look at the major cause of financial failure in the sports world - and in your world as well. We are going to do this by modeling a player's financial career and showing the slippery slope that leads to financial failure. At the end, it will be easy to see not only how quickly someone can go through a fortune of earnings, but also how it is practically inevitable.

Our fictitious player is "one of the smart ones." He realizes that he wants to spend appropriately and doesn't make any of the ridiculous purchases that are in the headlines. There is no zoo in his backyard, no Ferraris in his garage and no jewelry store in his master bedroom. He doesn't have a restaurant with his name on it. He does help his family, since his parents sacrificed everything working two jobs to get him to college. He has a couple of lifelong friends who helped him navigate the streets of his hometown, keeping him away from the gangs and the drug dealers so he could make it. Now that he has hit the big time, he will take care of them, but in a modest way. He is married with two kids and wants them to have all of the things that he never could provide otherwise, appropriate for his earning level. But he does not have a second family, an ex-wife or other personal money-draining relationships. In every way he did things the "right" way.

However, he is not a sophisticated investor and does not have any real investments. His major strategy is *"don't screw it up"*. He is an excellent saver and puts his money in the bank.

Fast Broke

If you think that $5 million, $20 million or even $100 million is a ticket to a lifetime free of financial woes, think again. If you come from a background where there wasn't much money at all, you might spend and spend and believe the money will never run out. It will. If you come from a background of scarcity, where money was saved, you might think that the savings will provide a secure existence. It won't. The lower return you get from your money, the lower your lifestyle will be. And the opposite is true as well. The higher return you get from your money, the higher your lifestyle can be.

One hundred million dollars sounds like an enormous amount of money. And it is. But what seems like an inexhaustible fortune can disappear all too fast. How can a person go broke on $100 million? It's all too easy to do. Let's use the popular example of the highly paid athlete. He finally gets that wonderful 10-year contract for $100 million. Here's how his money could evaporate. As you look this over, remember that I am actually being pretty conservative. To understand this, you have to start thinking like someone who believes his money is unlimited. He is not a business executive, attorney or any other type of professional. And the truth is that being a professional doesn't guarantee any type of financial success. For example, doctors are historically known to be terrible investors. Being smart at one thing doesn't mean you have the specific knowledge to be smart or successful at a different specialty activity such as investing.

But let's look at the math. The first lesson everyone learns with their initial paycheck is the difference between gross and net. The gross is the gigantic amount reported by the media when an athlete signs a new contract. He gets his first monstrous paycheck and sees all of the items automatically deducted from it. We all know that this is the money that we never get, as it goes right to our biggest business partner, the tax man. He gets all of the money you would pay in a divorce but never leaves you alone. He gets half of every paycheck, forever. And no matter how much you pay him, 98 percent of the rest of the world believes you should pay more. So don't expect your share to go down very often. The forces of government only push up.

So let's start with our figure of $100,000,000 over 10 years:

- ✓ $39,000,000 goes to federal taxes
- ✓ $7,000,000 goes to state taxes
- ✓ $1,450,000 goes to Medicare tax
- ✓ $4,000,000 goes to an agent (4% of gross earnings)
- ✓ $5,000,000 goes to a manager (5% of earnings)

That leaves $43,550,000- less than half the original amount - and he hasn't bought anything yet! Keep in mind that this figure does not account for a charitable giving plan or a tithe to a church, so another $10 million (10% of gross earnings) could easily be deducted.

Now let's examine what 10 years of big lifestyle looks like in some detail. I've seen lots of guys live this way and go broke a few years after reaching retirement. This happens not because they are such extravagant spenders, but because they don't know how to replace income. They build money-eating machines that can't be turned off and they don't have the fuel to keep them running. Remember that while this might look like an ostentatious lifestyle to you, it is not when compared to the income level.

To make the math easy to follow, we will assume that he pays for everything in full. Remember, he will earn this money over 10 years so he will be buying all of the items over time. Were he to finance some of the purchases – such as his home - he would still need to theoretically set aside enough money to generate the income to make the ongoing payments. So let's set that issue aside for now and call it a wash.

The first thing a player usually buys is his dream home. Assuming he is not in Los Angeles or New York, a reasonable figure for this is about $5,000,000. In most big cities, that will get you a really nice home of 8,000 to 10,000 square feet in the nicest area of town. Again, this is a reasonable purchase for a person with a $100 million contract. It is easy to go way above that in some cities. As all professional sports teams are in major cities, the real estate values in the most desirable areas of those cities will easily support this figure.

Rarely, however, does a player play for his hometown team, so he needs to have a home in the town where he plays. Remember, he is conservative, so he spends $3,000,000 on this home. This can get a little complicated as players are traded or switch teams via free agency. I have seen some players end up with nice real estate portfolios by ending up with homes in four cities, since luxury properties sometimes take a while to sell. But for simplicity's sake, let's assume the one home. Of course, for someone in this income bracket, it would be natural to have a vacation home. Let's add another $2,000,000 for that purchase. Now we have $10,000,000 of empty homes. We need to add another $5,000,000 for the furnishings for three homes. This will include everything that goes into a home: furniture and art, cars, audio and video equipment, jewelry, clothes and other toys. Remember, the stuff needs to be of the same quality as the house. You don't fill your mansion with stuff from Target and Wal-Mart.

And when on the receiving end of $100 million, even a rather conservative person will have some extravagance in their life, so let's set aside another $2 million. Keep in mind we are talking about a 10-year period. Subtract another $17,000,000, leaving our player with $26,550,000.

To review, all our $100 million man has done is paid his taxes and set up a couple of places to live. *And he has already gone through nearly 75 percent of his contract.*

What are some of the other obvious ways he will spend money? Typically, he will buy a house for his parents and family. When a player comes from a rough upbringing, he often will want to help his mother and father. So it is very common to buy them a house and furnish it to give them a better lifestyle. This will include a car, new wardrobe, spending money and all that goes with moving them to a nicer life.

And don't think that it stops with his parents. Often a player from a poor background will be the only one among his family and friends that is earning real money. How can you say no to a family member in trouble? Or a friend who can't make his rent or feed his kids? What do you tell a buddy about to go to jail for getting behind on child support payments? The pressure on a new millionaire from his family and friends can be enormous, and it often boils down to either helping them out or cutting them off. This is especially true of your family. Luckily, our player is pretty good at saying no, but he is taking care of a few buddies as we mentioned earlier. It is not a stretch to plug in another $2 million over 10 years.

Other things he will pay for include life insurance and legal bills (estate plan, home purchases, etc.) for another $1 million.

The original $100 million is down to $23,550,000 and he hasn't eaten a meal. Now he starts living his daily life. Below is a reasonable list of

Fast Broke

what a player will spend over a 10-year period. It is highly typical, and many of the expenses are the fixed costs of owning homes, being married and having kids. Others are typical for a high-income person. At the bottom of the list I will list some things *not* on the list that easily could be.

House expenses (10 years for 3 homes)

- Water bills — $ 48,000
- Utility bills — $ 240,000
- Property taxes — $1,000,000
- Homeowners Insurance — $ 200,000
- Property maintenance — $ 240,000

    TOTAL — $1,728,000

Let's assume that he is married with two kids in school. Here is a list of what he could easily spend over 10 years:

- Clothes — $1,000,000
- Jewelry — $1,500,000
- Hair/ Nails/ Spa — $ 100,000
- Personal Trainer — $ 400,000
- Personal Coach — $ 250,000
- Flowers — $ 100,000
- Private School (2 kids) — $ 750,000
- Nanny — $ 400,000
- Food at $300/day — $1,000,000
- Miscellaneous Expenses — $ 300,000
- Vacation/Travel — $1,000,000
- Mom/Dad/Family — $2,400,000
- Entourage Expenses — $2,400,000

    TOTAL (for 10 years) — $11,600,000

Fast Broke

This figure averages out to just under $100,000 per month in personal spending. This is not an outrageous sum of money under the circumstances. According to his contract, his gross income is almost a $1 million per month for 10 years. Add roughly $15,000 per month for house expenses, and his average monthly spending is about $111,000, or $1,300,000 per year.

Remember when I said there were several possible missing expenses? There is no figure here for child support or alimony for an ex-wife. There are no other relatives that he is supporting. There are no wild parties, multiple expensive cars, home recording studios, man caves, bad investments, extravagant jewelry, restaurants or bars, or any of the other things that inexperienced rich folk do every day that can add up to millions of dollars very quickly. There are hundreds of places that this scenario can get off track. The vast majority involve losing money, not making money. This is actually a best-case scenario.

So what happens when his career ends? He will be left with about $10,000,000 (or a lot less if he did any of the things listed above) and a lifestyle of $1,300,000 per year. That money will last him less than eight years - *if he has done everything right*. In real life, the forces pulling money out of his pockets are so strong, they are almost unstoppable. The reason that most players (or lottery winners, or even you) go broke is that they earn money and build a lifestyle based on it. When they are done playing, they have to have money to last 50-60 years with a lifestyle where their money will last 6-8 years, and that's if they were pretty good at saving. He is now on the slippery slope. He has a lifestyle to maintain with a good bit of money at the time he retires. So a race begins between learning how to earn enough money to maintain his standard of living and shedding his lifestyle.

How can he earn that kind of money? First, to maintain a $1.3 million per year lifestyle indefinitely, you must consistently earn in excess of $2.5 million a year before taxes. In the real world, that kind of money is earned by CEOs of billion-dollar companies, hedge fund managers, owners of large businesses and successful drug lords (the ones not in jail or dead). These are not the jobs athletes are qualified for when they stop playing. There are a few TV or coaching jobs that pay that level of money. However, those are notoriously difficult to land and short-lived. And to have a chance, the player has to earn that type of money every year.

What about investments? Remember that our player is not schooled in finance as a profession, so he needs to either keep it really simple or trust someone to do it for him. As you probably have heard, most businesses fail within five years. And that is when the owner knows what he is doing and works at it every day. Our sample player (who represents the vast majority) doesn't know how to run a successful business.

Let's say he decides to keep it simple and buy tax-free bonds returning 5 percent. Rates actually are closer to 2 percent, but it is only an example and I want to round in favor of our player having success. At 5 percent, he needs to invest and set aside a mere $26 million to pay for his lifestyle. Even if he invested his entire $10 million, he would have a $700,000 shortfall every year that would dwindle his savings. A buy and hold strategy in the stock market historically returns 10 percent annually - in theory. But here are a few problems. First, the 10 percent return is taxable. Second, the only way to live off it is to sell along the way, which consumes it. And there are times where the market takes a hit and requires years to recover. In those times, you will consume so much of your portfolio that the market will need to be a rocket ship for your account to replenish. So, you can see that neither of these strategies will get the job done. Your only real chance is to develop a strong business that will grow and provide income for a long time. But unfortunately, not many people are good enough business owners to do that, and most passive ownership opportunities pay the employees much more than the owner. And a failed business would reduce his earning power by another big chunk.

Maybe our player thinks he can sell two of his homes at a profit—but maybe where he lives, real estate values have plummeted. He is back where he started—and maybe worse. The higher a person lives, the lower he ends up when the money stops. The scary fact is that a lot of the expenses are going to continue, but there will be no way to pay for them. Maintaining the same comfortable lifestyle is going to be impossible. And this is for a person who is a good saver, lives a reasonable lifestyle and doesn't make any major mistakes. He is generous to his closest people, but not overly so.

Even that person is doomed to fail unless he can learn to be a highly successful investor or entrepreneur. Anyone can see by this example that failing is far easier than succeeding. And the chances of someone doing everything right are low. Don't underestimate the forces pulling money out of your pockets. It is enormous for you and the athlete. Nearly 70 percent of the American economy is driven by you buying stuff. That is called consumer spending. Many billions of advertising dollars are spent each year to convince you to swipe that card. The banks, financial services houses and even the Federal Reserve Chairman use every encouragement to get money in circulation. Remember Alan Greenspan encouraging people to use their house as a piggy bank? Our society and media encourage you to worship celebrities and buy useless items to look like them, smell like them, drive in luxury like them, even cut your hair like them. Remember

Fast Broke

"they" only teach you good advice *for them*. So the next time you read about an athlete or entertainer in bankruptcy, look behind the headline to see how it happened. Because it can happen to you, too!

Highly paid athletes are hardly the only people who fall into the "looking good" syndrome that rapidly depletes their resources. A cardiologist who earns half a million dollars a year may maintain a very cushy lifestyle that can be wiped out by malpractice suits. Inheritances are often regarded as gifts to be enjoyed, not invested. When they're gone, another one isn't likely to come along. When the money is used up, the extravagant lifestyle disappears. And where are you then? Step one is to start selling things. Your expensive furniture is now worth 10 cents on the dollar. Your nice car is down 50 percent in value if it is just three years old. Your expensive real estate is only available to other rich people, and if you are selling under pressure, the sharks will circle to get the property at a discount. They know that only a few people can afford the house, and if the market is slow, it is not unusual for a high-end home to sit for several years without selling while you are bled dry keeping it up. Everything you own is worth the least when you need it the most.

The real lesson is that whether you earn $100,000 or $100 million, it is never enough. Unless you can solve the long-term income problem, you are never secure. Your 401K looks great until you start drawing it down. Then you find out that you have been lied to by "projections." It isn't enough to last. Taxes are higher, your market returns are lower, and you don't spend less in retirement; you spend more. How can you not spend more? You have loads of free time, and everywhere you want to go or everything you want to do costs money. Want to travel, see the grandkids, and go golfing? Ka-ching! Very few investments actually create regular cash flow - except for the guy who sold it to

Fast Broke

you.

Chapter 9

You Were the Best There Is, So What's Next?

The first thing that hits you in the face when you retire is that you don't exist anymore. Most people - especially men - live in a world where "who they are" is "what they do." Ask most men - especially ball players - to tell you about themselves and the answer usually starts with "I'm a ball player" or "I was a ball player." They have always been a ball player and always will be. It has been a consuming feature of our lives for so long that it is what we are. It's not just a job we had for a while. It has provided everything in our lives for as long as we can remember.

There is almost no one that we associate with that doesn't know us from that life. We created our identity, met our friends, met our wives, and reveled in the life for so long that it defines us.

I remember when I retired, my wife and I were going through a rough patch and we decided to go to a personal development seminar called the Landmark Forum. It was a wild experience for me and the first time in my life that I really started to define myself as a person, not just as a ball player.

While we were doing a specific exercise, I had this experience of looking at myself from a perspective outside of me. I had this vision of myself as a large formal portrait, like one you would see in a European castle. It was a large canvas oil painting in an elegant gold frame.

The background of the portrait was the cumulative portrayal of my life. It was a collage of friends, family, my basketball career, my hobbies, etc. It was essentially all of the experiences from my life. The part of

Fast Broke

the portrait that was my face was a blank outline of me like the silhouettes that you had done at the State Fair when you were a kid. The face had no defining features like eyes, hair or a nose. And with a nose as big as mine, it's hard to believe that it wouldn't cast at least a shadow!

Anyway, the point that I got was that my identity was merely the aggregation of my life experiences. That is, *what I did*. If you removed the background of the portrait that was my life experiences, there was no "me" there. All that was left was a blank canvas. All I knew was what I did. I had no real idea of who I was. I was a ball player.

It actually was a very scary and disorienting experience once I realized that I had no real connection to who I was as a person. My life was so filled with wonderful things that I had no real need to dig deeper than that. Being a ball player was great.

The problem became real very quickly when one day I couldn't do that anymore. All of a sudden, there was no practice, no games, no playoffs, no road trips, no socializing around the games. Overnight, it was all gone.

I now had 24 hours a day to fill. I had no focus or motivation. After all, there was no training camp to be in shape for. There was no season to look forward to. No massive distraction called the NBA to fill up my days and nights. I suddenly had to create it all on my own. I instantly went from way in to all the way out. You find out quickly that you have little residual value when you aren't playing anymore.

Killing time

Structure disappears and you have 24 hours a day to fill. One of the issues in retirement that is totally misunderstood and rarely talked

Fast Broke

about is "what do you do all day?" You hear people say that they will finally have time to travel, spend time with their family, go golfing or stoke the fire of whatever hobby they have. Real life is rarely that way, though. For one thing, you have a lifelong routine that is difficult to break. Not because of personal rigidity, but because after so many years you adjust the elements of your daily routine to get things the way you like them. Plus, most people enjoy what they do. Of course, there is some segment that gets relief from years of hated work, but most people miss many things about their job, especially having a place to go to every day that gives them purpose.

For me, it meant that I had adjusted to the "seasonality" of my job. I got pumped up in the early fall anticipating the start of the season, and I fell into a funk in the early summer when the season ended. Fifteen years after my career ended, I still go through the same cycles every season. Even the daily cycle of six hours of sleep with an afternoon nap needed to be adjusted. Remember, I needed to be 100 percent ready to go at 7:30 p.m. most nights. And I still miss my naps.

Road trips were a perfect structure to have my private time to see a guy movie, read a book or balance the checkbook. With a family at home, it's much more difficult to carve out that time since there are always family responsibilities to take on.

Some things were perfect to do while held hostage on an airplane for two hours in the middle of a night after a game. I used to do all of those things that aren't more important than a family activity or more fun than hanging out at your kid's game. But I still miss having time carved out to get certain things done, without interruptions and guilt-free.

My wife still gets annoyed when we get on a plane and I go into "road trip mode," starting a book or some other activity when she sees it as a time that we can talk. See, being held hostage on a plane can work against you, too. (Don't tell her I said that!) And for her it is the same issue. There are plenty of times when she wishes that I had a road trip to go on so she could have her girl time.

Another thing for me is having workout time. It used to be part of the job to be in great physical shape all the time. I had a strict training regimen, including health care and regular massages. Motivation was no problem, since the immediate feedback to getting out of your routine was feeling like crap the next day when pushing yourself to the limit. Now, working out is a hobby. And with no training camp, upcoming games or the rush of the playoffs to look forward to, willpower is the main source of drive for getting it done.

And believe me, compared to inspiration and desire, willpower has its work cut out for it. To work out now means waking at 4:45 a.m. to get to the gym at 5:15. I have learned the hard way that if I don't work out before my family gets up, the chances of me finding a workout window are about 1 in 10. And if I don't get enough sleep, it is too easy to put it off until tomorrow. After all, I don't have a game coming up or anything. For someone who always had terrific willpower and discipline, this change is an unwelcome struggle.

One of the biggest emotional challenges in retirement is ending something at which you excelled. You have spent the better part of your entire life mastering a skill or becoming an expert in your field. In sports, you also have the feeling of being physically fit and the ability to do amazing things. Most athletes played their sport for several years before they began truly training to become a pro.

While you may imagine playing against LeBron James when you are 10 years old, it does not become a real thing until much later. And all of

Fast Broke

the hours spent on the playground aren't the same as being in the NCAA Final Four or sitting at the NBA draft waiting for your name to be called.

Many players have a ball in their hands for five years before they ever get coached. Then they are in the "funnel." You start as one of the millions of players at the YMCA or in an AAU program. Then you progress to be one of the million or so on a high school team. From there you flow through the funnel as one of the thousands that play on a college team. Finally, you get to the big time.

Each year there are about 50 openings in the NBA, which is the big time. And there are a few hundred players who play professionally somewhere else, either in a minor league, developmental league or one of the many foreign leagues. But believe me, no kid grows up dreaming of playing in Istanbul or Reno. The NBA is the destination. The other professional leagues are a steppingstone to the top, or a short-term thing until reality sinks in and a player decides to get on with his life.

So you made it through the process of climbing over the millions of kids that enter the funnel to become one of the 450 players in the world to make the NBA. You dodge injuries, legal traps, bad coaches, choking at the wrong time and any of the hundreds of other issues that can end your career before it starts.

You invest thousands of hours, make incredible sacrifices and endure physical exhaustion and pain. You know the pride that comes with meeting hundreds of challenges and conquering them all. You stand up to the withering pressure of daily "kill or be killed" competition. You know the extreme joy of victory and the deepest agony of defeat. (Does that sound familiar?)

Fast Broke

And then, it's over.

You left as the brain surgeon. Now you are the janitor

You had this incredible life experience of building a body of work. You (hopefully) loved what you did and that all of the effort was worth it. When you walked off the court you had mastered a skill so difficult that only one in a zillion get to do it at the highest level. You have single-mindedly dedicated a lifetime of work and effort to it.

And when you are done, you realize that almost none of that colossal effort translates into something useful in the "real world." I heard one person explain it this way: "You left the hospital as the brain surgeon and the next day you were the janitor."

It finally hits you and you realize that you are truly starting over. I don't mean starting over like rebuilding wealth after losing money like the musician Billy Joel did. Facing financial problems, he went back on tour for a couple of years and rebuilt his wealth. What I mean is re-entering the world looking up at Mt. Everest and having never climbed a mountain.

In your mind, you look at success as having achieved it on the highest level. So you want to climb Mt. Everest, you believe you can climb Mt. Everest and your ego demands it. The problem is that you don't have enough skill to climb a sand dune. You took for granted the effort and time it took to master your sport and make it to the top. But having made it there once, you know what it is like at the top. And you liked it. You also believe you can do it. The problem is committing the time and effort to achieving the level of skill that you had in your sport.

As we discuss the issues that we all face in retirement, I found that the intangible is more impactful than the tangible. Purpose, passion, professional skill and pride are among the most difficult things to replace. The tangible things like money, lifestyle and friendships all become by-products of the intangibles.

This very important issue is another example of the "left foot first" concept. So many of us try to fill the void in our lives created by losing our professional identities that we rush out looking to do something without regard to how we intend to satisfy our intangible needs.

After all, how can we expect to pick a new endeavor if we don't have any direction?

Fast Broke

Fast Broke

Chapter 10

The Spam Hits The Fan

After I was downsized from playing in the NBA, I decided to get on with life. As I mentioned earlier, I continued in media as the color analyst for Seattle Super Sonics telecasts while my wife and I did seminar education to develop the needed skills for my life as an investor and entrepreneur.

Over the next seven years, I used the principles I learned as an athlete to develop my investing skills:

- I studied and learned my fundamentals
- I practiced to master my skills
- I hired quality coaches
- I built a strong team
- I started small
- As I got better I did more
- I used my statistics to measure my progress and results

Over those next seven years, we went from flipping single-family homes to developing a small residential subdivision to participating in large apartment complexes and condominium conversions. During that time, we bought and sold over 1,000 residential units.

We focused on strong fundamentals. For example, we made sure that the properties we kept all had large equity positions, about 30 percent or more. We knew that the home market was softening and wanted to make sure we had plenty of cushion.

We also only bought great properties in the best areas. When things

Fast Broke

go bad, the best properties hold their value better than the average ones and we wanted as many things in our favor as possible.

We were confident that we knew the real estate market well and had built a strong portfolio of properties. When the market crash happened in 2008, we found out some interesting things.

We were in the process of building a home for resale on a site in the Denver suburb of Greenwood Village. We had a construction loan with Washington Mutual that would automatically convert to a permanent loan when the building process was completed. When that happened in the summer of 2007, we had trouble with the process. It turned out that WaMu has screwed up our paperwork and never sent us the conversion documents.

For three months we sent in the agreed-upon payments, waiting for the final documents to be processed so we could sell the home. We had an equity position over $1 million and were looking forward to getting paid. When the documents were finally delivered, we were shocked to see that they sent us a foreclosure package. It turns out that instead of converting our loan, the bank took our payments, never credited the loan and reported us as delinquent! We were outraged.

So instead of perfect credit, we now had major black marks on our credit report. While they promised to fix it, all they did was stall while the parent company went bankrupt at the start of the credit crisis of 2008. So now I was forced to sell the house while fighting a wrongful foreclosure against a bankrupt lender. As you can imagine, buyers started playing hardball as they thought we were in financial trouble.

Now my false 90-day late was reported to all of the credit agencies. Overnight, all of my credit cards, lines of credit, and business credit

Fast Broke

were shut off. It is tough to run any business without revolving credit. So here we were, entering the credit crisis at a time where we had credit mistakes from a bankrupt bank, essentially destroying 20 years of perfect credit practices.

I immediately called my bank representatives to see what I needed to do to fix this. I had always been a great customer, never missed a payment, and wanted to keep my relationships strong. Remember, at this time no one knew what was going to happen. Even the banks didn't have any idea what they were doing at this point.

The only advice they would give me was to stop paying my mortgages. They would not be able to talk to me if I was current on my loans. They explained that they had so many delinquent loans to deal with that all of their resources were tuned into that. Customers who were current were not to be dealt with.

What kind of system is that? You refuse to talk with your good customers to concentrate on the bad ones? With that, we started on the path of figuring out the credit crisis. Our large equity positions disappeared quickly as home values in some of the top areas in the country collapsed to unheard-of levels.

Isleworth Country Club in Orlando, Florida is one of the most highly rated areas in the country. Values dropped 50 percent in three months. In Paradise Valley, Arizona, the premier community in the state, values dropped an astounding 70 percent.

We quickly learned the value of a great financial education. While the vast majority of folks just gave up and surrendered their homes to the bank, we decided to work it out. During my education process, I learned many things about property rights, notes and liens, deeds and loans etc. I knew enough to recognize that the banks were literally stealing homes they did not have the right to. We fought the banks through negotiating and the courts. We sued some of the largest and most powerful lenders in the world. We had a great team of attorneys who were outraged at how the court system favored the banks over the homeowners to the point of ignoring many points of law.

The bankers tried many dirty tricks against us to illegally foreclose properties. Luckily we were educated enough to see what they were doing and stop them. After seven years, we finally came out on top and were one of the very few homeowners who were able to win against the banks. We even have a ruling named after us that now requires the courts to follow the laws that favor homeowners.

Through it all we found the power to come out on top by using the sports model to achieve success in our other endeavors. While we are more convinced than ever that the financial system is designed for people to fail, by taking responsibility for your own results and using the skills and techniques that we have shared, anything is possible.

Winning results become achievable by understanding how the system works, not just by memorizing information. The power of teamwork, great coaching, powerful analysis and commitment will see you through to success. Remember that when markets are rising and everything you do works, it is easy to think that you are smarter than you really are. When the Spam hits the fan, you really find out what you are made of.

And sooner or later, it will.

Fast Broke

Chapter 11

Create a Structure To Use

When I started on the path to entrepreneurship, I immediately noticed that I needed to create my world. This wasn't like getting a job where you would show up at work and plug yourself into their system. Whatever I needed, I had to build from scratch. In the information age, there was no shortage of "How To" manuals full of specific information on any possible topic. I studied at many seminars to learn the information I needed to complete different tasks. I studied how to buy and sell houses, trade stocks, create entities, grow as a person and many more useful topics. The problem was that I would get jammed up as soon as I started to take a specific action.

My first problem was my desire to get on with it and *do something*. I wanted action and results. This is how I operated my entire life - with action and results. I finally realized what was missing. I needed a structure and model on which to base my business systems. I needed to start at the very beginning. I had always been part of a team. When I looked at it even deeper, I realized that my team was part of a larger team that was within an even larger system.

The team I played on was made up of coaches, trainers and players with specific skills that were designed to do one thing: win games. That team was part of a bigger team called the franchise. There were many other people that sold tickets, marketed the product, negotiated television deals, ran the arena, and so on. All of that operated within a huge machine called the league. It was made up of a larger team that coordinated the efforts of 30 franchises that each had their own teams within them. I really got to marvel at the layers of coordination and skill that it took to make the machine work.

Fast Broke

I had to figure out how to build something that would work for me. I realized that to build a successful operation from scratch, I needed to examine everything that I believed and open my understanding of the *big* picture. I was used to existing as my part of this giant system. Now I had to generate it myself. So I started at the beginning.

What model do I use?

Even with this realization, I still had trouble getting going. I hadn't yet stepped back far enough to see the entire picture. Before I could build the framework, I needed to figure out what model I was going to use. As I was working to figure it out, I naturally could only see what I knew existed. What I knew was "to do-ing." So I started. I generated a lot of activity with the anticipation of creating this really cool thing. I quickly realized that I had trouble making certain decisions. The smallest thing would trip me up and all my momentum would just stop. One day it hit me like a ton of bricks.

After much frustration, I realized that I didn't have a model to follow. My actions were creating an inconsistent collection of parts without coherency. I was essentially making it up as I went along. If there was ever a recipe for failure, I was following it. I desperately needed a plan to follow. I knew of many successful businesses in the world, so it seemed like a simple thing: Just do what they were doing.

I figured that there was no reason to reinvent the wheel. It already was round; I didn't need to make it rounder. There were many successful people out there with hundreds of books on the subject. Surely the answer I was looking for was in one of those. So I started looking and reading. I studied the biggies: Warren Buffett, Bill Gates, Donald Trump, Richard Branson and others. They each had different paths to success and lots of advice. But I didn't find what they did to be reproducible.

The advice was pretty general, and their circumstances were all very unique in their own way. Plus, very few people have the unique combination of factors to achieve the kind of tremendous success that they did. They built businesses that employ thousands of workers and have access to assets that are unimaginable to most people. Their companies have layers and layers of managers to generate work output to keep these colossal machines growing and thriving. The vast majority of people need to start at the beginning and have a clear path to follow to get traction.

So where did the answer actually lie? What was the model I could understand clearly, implement easily and follow through to results? I kept looking. What about successful companies like Apple with Steve Jobs, or General Electric with Jack Welch? These examples have been studied, analyzed, and put under the microscope. Again, these massive results are as much a product of a driving force that was unique and not easily reproducible. Steve Jobs was a one-in-a-billion visionary that changed the world. They broke the mold when they made him. Of course, that's the problem. We need the mold.

I finally realized that the answer wasn't trying to copy a person or company that was once-in-a-millennium successful. No one else can really do it. After all, I didn't pattern my game after Michael Jordan's, either. Why bother? I didn't have the skills that he had.

After much contemplation, I realized I was a master of the most proven success model ever created: how to succeed at professional sports.

Sports provide the most used, analyzed, tweaked and repeated success model in existence. It is the most applicable to people because most individuals can manage a group the size of a sports team versus one the size of Microsoft. And even if you are not a sports person, the elements are understandable. I found that it was fairly easy to break down the sports experience and compare it to an individual's needs in life in a clear and understandable way.

Why all sports analogies are wrong: What are the real keys?

It's hard to get very far without hearing a sports analogy about a topic. Do you want to "quarterback your team"? Do you ever "punch above your weight," or "cross the finish line?" The last thing you want to do is "fumble on the one-yard line!"

But the reality is that in the world of investing and success, most sports analogies are dead wrong. The last thing you want to be is the quarterback of the team or think like a head coach. You don't even want to be the general manager.

All of those positions get a lot of attention, but those jobs are where small thinking happens. Each of those positions is just one small part of a bigger machine. And worst of all, those positions are expendable with a notoriously short life span.

The quarterback is a producer for someone else. He gets beat up much of the time and if he doesn't produce every game he gets replaced. Does that sound like a formula for success?

What about the head coach? Doesn't he get to make the decisions during the game? Well, sort of. Actually, he is really a middle manager. He is under the general manager who picks the players and makes the trades. He works with what he has and is the first one fired when things go bad.

Fast Broke

Ah, then you certainly want to be the general manager. He is the one who really makes the decisions, right? After all, he picks the players, hires the coach and makes the trades. In truth, he has all of the responsibility but no real authority. He gets to keep his job as long as he makes all of the right moves. If he makes one major mistake, he gets canned.

Well, who then?

When I work with players, the first thing I discuss with them is that they need to start thinking like the one person they have the least understanding of: the *owner*. The owner has the ultimate say in all decisions, the ultimate responsibility for the outcome, and all of the benefits when things work out well. (And yes, all of the problems when things don't.) When a team wins the championship, the commissioner gives the trophy to the owner, not the star player, coach or general manager.

The biggest shift any one has to make is that he is the *owner* of his life. He is responsible for his outcome. He hires his GM (his business advisor). He is responsible for picking his strategists (coaches), producers (players) and the rest of his team. He oversees the action, grades the performance and sets up his accountabilities.

The bottom line is that whatever happens, good or bad, is his outcome. There is no one to blame. The biggest shift most people have to make is to take ownership of their lives. The vast majority of people typically waive responsibility for their lives and give it to someone else. It might be their company, the government or their stockbroker.

If there is one universal lesson in sports, it is that we are each responsible for our own results. This is clearly obvious for individual athletes. There is nowhere to hide for a golfer or tennis player. But even team athletes know they have individual responsibility that is part of the team's success.

A Game of Mistakes

In every sport, mistakes are made. The idea, especially in team sports, is not so much that you play a mistake-free game, but that you learn from your mistakes. The key is that your mistakes are smaller than your successes. The things you do well outweigh the things you do wrong. We all make mistakes.

We have a saying in sports: *Don't let one mistake become two mistakes.* If you miss a shot, don't stand there and yell at the referee while your guy goes down and scores. Or if the referee missed a call, don't foul your man at the other end because you're pissed off. Now you've made a second mistake.

You have to understand that investing is imperfect, and living your life is an imperfect thing. Mistakes are going to be made, and you can't let them dominate the conversation. When you make them, learn from them and move on. Focus on the things you're doing right. Frankly, mistakes and failures teach you a lot of valuable lessons you may not have learned without trying. I used to tell people that if you're not making mistakes, you're not trying hard enough. If you're doing everything right, that means you're only doing the few limited things you know how to do well. You're not taking on bigger challenges or growing or looking for bigger opportunities.

Most athletes will tell you that you learn much more from your mistakes than from your successes. We tend to examine mistakes more, and most people experience the pain of mistakes more than the joy of doing it right. Winners know that failing is a crucial part of success. After all, everything we know at one point was foreign to us.

So embrace mistakes as a key to becoming a winner.

We all know that sports also provide valuable life lessons that are universal. Sports teach us how to compete, work as part of a team, accept responsibility, learn new skills, pursue excellence, and many others. Another reason that sports is such a valuable success system is that beyond serving as a metaphor, sports provide a complete range of success principles.

Fast Broke

Chapter 12

Most People Come From a Place of Lack, Not Abundance

Most people are trained from birth to live in a society built on consuming, not growing. We receive literally millions of messages in our lifetimes that teach us strategies to separate us from our money. We are taught to buy plenty of items that lose value the minute we swipe the card. Most of what we are told are "investments" (mutual funds, real estate, etc.) are really high-risk savings accounts over which you have little or no control. The wealth strategies you learn are really wealth strategies for the person selling you the product.

Very few people have the opportunity to learn true wealth creation. It is not taught systematically to our population. And the very institutions that profit from selling you a product or service provide the vast majority of the information that is available. It should come as no surprise that the information you rely on to make an investment decision is biased in favor of the seller, not you. When you see the statistics proving that an overwhelming number of hard-working, well-meaning people work their entire lives only to retire broke, you have to realize that the game is rigged from the start.

Even more difficult to navigate is the path from poverty to wealth. While individual stories of people doing it abound and America is known as "The Land of Opportunity," only a small percentage of people complete this difficult trek. The system is just not designed for very many people to really make it. While the top basketball players make gazillions of dollars, millions of players enter the system to compete for the 500 jobs that make that money. Tom Cruise may make $20 million for one movie, but less than 10 percent of working actors make a full-time living at acting. And I am pretty sure you have heard that 90 percent of businesses fail within five years.

So it is easy to see why so few people have real experience related to being wealthy. However, most people have plenty of broke friends.

To start with, most people in America were raised and educated by poor people. Only small percentages of people are truly financially free, or grew up in a home of abundance (having more than you need). Most of us grow up longing for all the cool junk we see on TV, in stores or on LeBron James' feet. When all you know about money is that you can buy stuff with it, it makes the transition from lack to abundance pretty difficult. Forget about information; the first thing you need to learn is how to break the emotional addiction to wanting things. When you finally make this tremendous emotional breakthrough, you are ready to become financially educated.

The level of financial education in this country is actually pretty low. While the amount of information is large and easily available on the Internet, the content is pretty well controlled by the institutions. As a result, the information is largely of the "what they want you to think and know" variety. In addition, it is common to hear totally conflicting opinions from "experts" on TV and in the media. It is hard to know what to do with the overabundance of "advice," especially since it is typically not in any useful context. One of the strategies used very successfully by the industry is to make the process seem so complicated and difficult that you feel lost and overwhelmed. You think that you need to rely on a professional to handle things rather than actually learn it yourself. The other message that is drilled into us from childhood is to buy stuff - lots of stuff - early and often. When you couple the desire to acquire with seemingly unlimited credit cards, it is no wonder we spend more than we make. Even the government depends on the miracle of "deficit spending." It repeatedly shows us it can raise the debt ceiling, spend more money it doesn't have and promise to manage this growing cancer sometime in the future. It doesn't have an actual plan to handle the growing debt and in fact show us that a winning plan is to lower the rate at which we add to this deficit. Starting to chip away at the debt is at least 10 years away.

The major result of these conflicting sets of messages is that people rely on the financial strategy of spending and buying rather than saving and investing. Investing is complicated, after all. And you might go crazy looking at your account with the way the markets swing back and forth. You will hear that you are better off leaving it alone for decades, not trying to manage your money. It is much easier to spend than save; it is something we all know how to do. It is no wonder that the vast majority of Americans have little or no savings, a retirement account that is not performing very well, and an inadequate retirement looming. Then the lack continues.

Building a Lifestyle

People and players don't build a lifestyle overnight. It happens in a gradual way, more of a slippery slope. Remember, athletes have a compressed timeline for everything and get to it quicker and harder than most people, but the mechanism is pretty much the same. Building a lifestyle usually happens in fits and starts. With the first contract, a player usually does a quick binge on the things he has wanted for a long time. The list is pretty much what you would expect:

- Cars
- House and furnishings
- Complete wardrobe
- Adult toys (home theatre, electronic gizmos, etc.)

Fast Broke

- House and furnishings for mom

You get the point. With the NBA's rookie salary scale, there is a limit on the first wave of spending. However, it is natural for a player with a multi-year contract to be able to overspend, since any lender will give credit on future guaranteed income. This will allow an undisciplined athlete to get ahead of his checks. Plus, a player in the early stage of his career steps totally unprepared into the system that is designed to separate him from his money. This system is complete, thorough and much better at getting money out of a player's pocket than a player is at getting money into his savings.

At this point, though, there are some factors that ratchet up the spending that have not yet come into play. For instance, very few young players are married. Spending for two is much more than double the cost of spending for one. So the single guys - even if they have a kid - spend less than the married guys. Very few players' wives work. This is because of a combination of the player's high income, the natural mechanism of few players playing where they want to live, and the unsteady nature of a player's lifestyle. I know when I changed teams a few times, it pretty much killed my wife's TV career.

Another factor slowing initial spending is that a player from a poor background quickly passes a level of living he knows nothing about. He has never dealt with an expensive home, developed an interest in art or sculpture, or shopped at high-end furniture stores. It takes some time to grow into these types of tastes. But sooner or later he will, and that's when the lifestyle can really accelerate. It is difficult to balance the growing lifestyle with the future income. There is no way to know what the future holds, but there are a lot of pressures to add more people and things to the growing spending. It is pretty inevitable for the spending to get ahead of the earning.

Fast Broke

Why do we keep up with the Joneses (and the O'Neals)?

One of the biggest emotional pulls regarding your money is keeping up with the Joneses. That is when people spend money on things for other people to see them using, wearing, driving, etc., regardless of whether it makes sense - or if they even want it. In the NBA and other professional sports, this game reaches stratospheric heights as large budgets meet big egos. I remember when I was first in the league, I lived in Salt Lake City, which did not have a good big man's clothing store. When we went on the road to cities that had one of the top stores, every guy over 6-6 would go clothes shopping. As you can imagine, having a herd of tall guys all shopping at the same time was quite a sight. One of the most common problems was that the store would not typically stock six of the same item, say a specific shoe, in the same size. So there was quite a frenzy about who got what when something really stylish was seen.

The next problem was one you typically only see on a red carpet at the Oscars. We have all heard about the dilemma of two women showing up at the same event in the same dress. That is one of the biggest fashion *faux pas* possible. Believe me, it is no different when two 7-footers show up at a game in identical sweaters. You cannot believe the locker room ribbing. Players are as conscious of what each guy is wearing as women at a party. Their egos get into it, and the trash-talking is brutal. Try showing up to a game with pants that are too short or wearing an ugly sweater and see what happens.

My former teammate Darrell Armstrong once came to a playoff game wearing a yellow suit. He was not on the active roster and sat on the bench for a game that was nationally televised. The broadcasters had a field day, and he got talked about as much as some of the guys playing in the game. The teammates gave him so much crap about it that he auctioned off the suit for charity. The good news was he was a popular player and the suit brought a nice price! Once, I wore these wonderful tailored winter white slacks to a game in Milwaukee. Once. Boy, did I hear about it. In Orlando, I had a light blue suit that made the newspaper and started a feud with another player with whom I thought I was pretty close. I need to call him to see if we are still feuding, because I haven't talked to him since. Really.

Whether in the suburbs or an NBA locker room, we are all conscious of the other guy's car, house, clothes, jewelry, etc. And don't forget the wives - they have their own contest going on. Sometimes it is tough to tell whose issues are bigger. When I was with the Lakers, Elden Campbell showed up one day in the newest, high-end Mercedes exactly like the one Magic Johnson drove. It was seen as too pricey for anyone but Magic, but he had to have one.

None of us are immune. And the bigger the budget, the bigger the mistakes that can be made. It is a challenge sometimes to keep guys from getting priced right out of their earnings. I always tell the young guys that they don't have Shaquille O'Neal's budget, so don't even start. The veteran superstars can afford a lot of stuff that you can't, so be smart. Sometimes they listen, and sometimes they don't.

Don't drown in the bathtub

The mechanism by which many athletes and millions of Americans go broke can be easily visualized by a metaphor of a large bathtub. For top athletes, the tub is better represented by a swimming pool. But for now let's keep it a large tub. The faucet represents our earned money. The more we earn, the more water is pouring into the tub. Of course, the drain represents our expenses. As we earn more, the faucet pours out more and more water, filling the tub. As we spend more, the drain gets bigger and bigger, letting more water out and lowering the level. That is our cash flow. I am using this example only to represent cash flow, not net worth. Cash flow is the most important figure in determining a person's ability to live comfortably, not net worth. After all, it doesn't matter what you own if you can't pay your bills, does it?

Look at the water in the tub. As we earn more than we spend, the water level rises. When we spend more than we earn, the water level drops. While this is a simple example, it is a tremendous visualization of your cash flow.

What trips up most athletes who fail is not the uncontrollable spending that burns up entire contracts quickly (although it certainly happens quite spectacularly for some). What typically gets guys is when they earn a lot of money, create a large lifestyle, and then retire with a good chunk of money in the bank. They have a large tub filled with water with the drain wide open. As long as the faucet of income is on, the tub remains relatively full. But when the faucet is shut off, the drain isn't very easy to close.

They have a large home and its expenses, kids to support at a high level, etc. The drain seems to get bigger, and water rushes out. They have to find a way to open the faucet and get more water pouring in. They also need to slow the drain by cutting things out. Usually it is a race to see which happens first.

Many players have it figured out when a crash happens, or a deal goes bad. For some, it can simply mean that interest rates go down and their interest income no longer covers their monthly expenses. What about working? As many people find out when they have a life transition, it is tough to find a job that pays CEO money when your skill set doesn't have anything to do with business. Athletes actually have a similar experience to newly divorced stay-at-home moms. They try to enter the workforce after being out of the market for 10-plus years, competing with people with contemporary, specific experience. It can be tough to turn that faucet on high.

What has that got to do with me, you ask? Remember that athletes are just an exaggerated version of you. They retire earlier, but you will have the same issues later on. Money managers will try to explain that you will spend less in retirement than when you are working. In real life, you now have 40-60 hours a week to fill that you didn't have before. What do you plan on doing for that amount of time that doesn't cost money? What about traveling to see the grandkids, or golfing, or getting out of bed? It all costs money. So look at your own tub to see where the faucet will be turned on.

It will never happen to me. Or will it?

Most players listen politely when they hear stories from former players but believe it will never happen to them. They see their situation differently. Maybe they believe that they make more money, so they will be fine. Or they trust their agent to do the right thing for them. Or they will be smarter and not overspend. Or they don't have a lot of kids or extended family to support. The sad truth is that they can do everything "right" and still fail. When you look at the system in detail, you will recognize it is designed to help you fail more than it is designed to help you succeed. You will start to look past the sales pitch and see the underlying lie behind it. You will see how the miracle of projections is dangerous at best and a flat-out scam at worst.

It takes a dedicated person who is constantly vigilant to make it. It is no easy task to navigate the propaganda waters that pass for financial information in America today. Want a simple example on how you can

Fast Broke

do everything "right" and still lose your shirt? Look no further than the fixed income market. Ten years ago, you wanted something that you could count on to pay a safe income. You invest $10 million at 6.5 percent in a safe product. It is paying you $650,000 per year, so you feel confident you can maintain your lifestyle. Now you learn that for the last five years, interest rates have dropped, and now you are making $200,000 per year.

Plus, your quality rental real estate has gone down in value by 40 percent and now is less than worthless. Your stock portfolio went down by half, but luckily you didn't panic sell and now it recovered to about where it was. Unfortunately, the dollars it brings you are really only worth about 60 cents each compared to 10 years ago. But if you listen to the news, there is no inflation. Especially when they only count the items they want to and not the items that actually went up.

Here's your situation: You are cash flow negative, your real estate is lost, your net worth went down by a big chunk in real terms and you are depleting your savings. And what did you do to deserve this? You were a good saver, bought terrific properties in the best areas and invested with a conservative strategy in the stock market. All of the things that you were told were the "right" things to do. Does any of this sound familiar to millions of people in America right now? Aren't you glad that you did all of the "right" things?

One typical mistake many athletes make is putting the proverbial cart before the horse. In this case, it means depending on the next contract as a rationalization for not saving money now. It is so easy in any player's career to have a strong belief in the next contract.

For the most part, a player with a solid game in a productive situation can expect something good to happen when his contract is up. There are examples on every team of guys getting big deals. However, there are lots of reasons why a deal might not happen. Injury is the biggest. Lightning can strike with a torn knee ligament or a blown disc in the back. Plus, sometimes a good player just doesn't find a place. There are only a certain number of roster spots, and you can count on 50 going to rookies each year. That means that an equal number of veteran players must disappear through retirement, injury or losing the highest paying musical chairs game in the world.

Each year it is painful to see guys waiting for a deal and watching the contracts getting signed. One by one, the remaining spots dry up, especially for some of the salary-protected exemption spots. A player can get in trouble pretty quickly if he is not prepared to sit out a season or take a large pay cut. There are many players who don't know that they "retired." They just get cut and have a hard time getting back into the league.

In the business world the story is the same, just multiplied by a few thousand. All over America, companies are downsized and it often catches people off guard. Those who have a lifestyle that has them living paycheck to paycheck can get into a world of hurt quickly. They must also be prepared to survive a dry spell or accept a pay cut.

The good news is that the same skills players mastered to become great in sports can be used to solve their retirement problems. So can you. In the next two chapters, I will discuss in detail some of the most important and universal principles that make sports such a powerful success system to adopt.

Enjoy!

Chapter 13

Always Know the Score

Of all of the features that make sports such a popular pastime, one of the absolute keys is the thoroughness at which all sports keep and analyze statistics. No matter what the sport, the vast array of measures and the effort put into analyzing those measures is what separates sports from any other endeavor.

It's no wonder that the appeal of sports is so universal. The fact that it is so completely recorded and analyzed makes it accessible to everyone. All you need to do is look at the explosion of fantasy leagues across all sports to see that the vast majority of folks competing in sports never get off the couch.

Riddle: Which is the only sport where no knows the score until the event is over? Neither the players, fans, coaches or referee have any way to measure who is ahead while the event is going on. Hint: This lack of transparency also makes it the most corrupt sport. The answer is at the end of the chapter.

What it is about statistics and scorekeeping that makes sports endure through the centuries?

First of all, just the fact that the score is kept and displayed ignites our competitive juices. All athletes know that when you practice without keeping score, it gets boring really quickly. Even a simple activity such shooting baskets can be tedious and uninspiring if you just shoot without keeping track of your makes and misses. And anyone who has hit tennis balls back and forth with a friend knows how boring it is until you start keeping score.

Fast Broke

Keeping track of your outcome makes you try harder!

The second reason to keep score is to know if you are doing it right. By always knowing the score, you have constant feedback on how you are doing. In a game, the score is the ultimate measure of your performance. That figure is what is used to determine who won or lost. In business, cash flow is usually the key indicator of how well a company is doing. The same holds true for your personal finances. At the end of the month, how will you know if you had a good month? Look at the score - in this case, your monthly cash flow.

In sports and business, keeping accurate measures and statistics are crucial to success. The key is to know which measures are important and which ones are not.

The biggest key to why sports is such a powerful success model is the commitment that sports makes to measuring performance, figuring out which measures are important and constantly analyzing those measures in real time.

That allows for continuing adjustments to improve performance on a consistent basis.

Let's take a minute to look over how a basketball team tracks statistics, analyzes them in real time and uses that information to improve performance during a game. We will also compare how you might do the same thing in your life. Remember, the key is not only to gather data, but also to analyze it in a useful way so you can act on the information.

The first thing a team does is committing to using stats in a meaningful way. They hire specialists to record data and present it in a certain way for analysis. They have a predefined set of measurements that are taken, put into a stat sheet and continuously distributed to the coaching staff. The information is available in real time throughout the game.

For an individual, it is important to work with your accountant and/or bookkeeper to set up what expenses you need to measure and create a spreadsheet that can be easily updated and viewed. You will need to track money in and out (cash flow), tax deductible expenses (including mortgage interest), depreciation expenses and other key measures. The good news is that with current accounting software and mobile apps, you can keep these measures in real time, just like your favorite team.

Now what good are measures if you don't look at them? Do you ever notice at a basketball game how at the beginning of every timeout, the coaches huddle to look over the stat sheet *before* talking to the players? They are looking for a significant statistic to see if they need to make a strategy adjustment or a substitution.

How often do you look over your financial stats to see how things are going? You spend money every minute of every day in some form or another. You eat, start your car, run your air conditioner, go shopping, etc. How much better would your financial picture be if you really understood what was happening with your money more often? Do you look at your finances at least as often as you watch "The Bachelor?"

Another key feature with sports is that teams call timeout. When things aren't going well, the coach simply calls a timeout to regroup. He takes a minute, talks to his advisors and team and thinks things through. In addition, he is forced to take a longer break at the end of each quarter and at halftime. The key is that he has predetermined times where he stops and looks at his performance and makes adjustments if needed.

Most of us just plow through our lives with little or no time taken for reflection. How often do we really sit and analyze our situation with our advisors, family members or mentors to keep updated on things? Do you meet with you accountant once a year to do your taxes? Did you do it in June to plan for the end of the year, or did you just bring him the receipts in February when it was too late to do anything?

How often do you sit with your family to discuss your spending habits, future needs, etc.? Ever? You can learn from your favorite team that it only takes a minute to see the picture and keep on the right track.

This just covers the most basic statistical work. Most pro sports teams now do very advanced analytics. Just like coaching, professional teams realize that the more serious they become the bigger commitment they make to analyze everything they do. They strive to identify the most useful measures and use them to make constant adjustments to their mix in search of maximum performance.

For many of us, hiring a complete staff to analyze our personal business may be impractical. After all, we don't have the $100 million budget for our own business. However, it is important to remember that stats don't lie. The better information we get, the more we review and understand the numbers, and the more we take action based on real information, the better results we are going to get.

I am willing to bet that the cost of a good accountant, bookkeeper and some accounting software will be paid for at least double in tax savings, more efficient spending and reduced therapist bills. Nothing is more stressful personally and to a marriage than money problems. The vast majority of people who don't invest the time and money

Fast Broke

necessary to master this part of their lives amaze me.

I have tried it both ways. When I have been diligent in mastering my money, my life has been full of clarity and ease. During the periods of my life when I lost some control, the exact opposite has been true. That's how I know the level of stress that is caused by not keeping it under control. I've lived it.

Answer to the riddle: Boxing. In boxing, the fighters, fans, referees and managers just have to guess who is ahead during the fight. There is no scoreboard displaying the score, no stat sheet breaking down the action. The ringside announcers have more information than the competitors do. It is no surprise that boxing had been plagued by scandals and corruption. It is easiest to manipulate the outcome when no one can track the score during the fight.

Fast Broke

Fast Broke

Chapter 14

Everyone Has a Coach

If there is one factor that athletes understand better than any other, it is the importance of coaching. It is virtually unthinkable in any sport for a player to operate without a coach. With very few exceptions, every team and player on every level has a coach. Team sport athletes cannot imagine playing a game without a coach. Individual athletes also have one or more coaches, even in sports such as tennis which prohibit contact with the coach during the contest.

In fact, it is so common that all athletes take for granted that they have coaching as a constant and permanent part of their lives. Many go to great lengths to select a specific coach or choose a specific team based on the coach. Many gymnasts for example will move to a new city to train with a specific coach. And on the higher levels, it is not just one coach but a team of coaches operating in concert to create a coaching experience covering all aspects of an athlete's life.

Each type of activity will necessitate the type of coaching needed, as will the skill level and budget. After living a professional life with heavy coaching, it is hard for me to imagine a coachless existence. As a matter of fact, when I have taken on an endeavor on my own, I have usually struggled or failed. When I have had quality coaching, my outcome has always been much better. Having a coach is not a guarantee of success by itself, but it makes a huge difference in the outcome.

Yet in real life, very few people have coaching as a regular part of their daily lives. Most people experience life by trying to figure it out on their own. Even when coaching is involved, it is sporadic in nature and not as complete as it could be. We have many reasons (or excuses) for not having a coach. Maybe it's the feeling that it costs money, or possibly not knowing where to look. It could be as simple as not realizing the true value of quality coaching. Whatever it is, remember that the most successful people truly understand the value of coaching, and the most proven success model out there – sports – relies heavily on coaching.

As we learn to approach our lives like a game that needs to be won, it easy to see how our lives can be enhanced if we took the same approach to coaching that successful athletes and sports teams do.

Another interesting fact is that there is never a time in an athlete's life where they feel they no longer need coaching. As a matter of fact, as athletes get better and better, they normally increase their use of coaching rather than decrease it. They are constantly looking for an edge. Many top athletes look to add specialty coaches to develop a specific element in their game.

In basketball, it might be a shot coach to work on adding a specific move. LeBron James, the best basketball player in the world, spent a summer working on his post-up game. Even though he is a guard and not a center, he wanted to add that skill to his arsenal of offensive moves. He hired Hall of Fame center Hakeem Olajuwon to work with him on that very specific part of his game.

When Tiger Woods was the top-ranked player in the world, he hired a new swing coach to revamp his game. What's better than No. 1 in the world? He felt he could improve even more. Did he sit there and try to figure it out on his own? Of course not. He hired a coach to travel with him and work on his swing.

The point is that 'the best' understand the value of coaching better than anyone. They are constantly looking to improve with the help of great coaching. How many of us in our day-to-day lives rely on coaching on that level? Not many. Do you think that these top athletes might be on to something? We accept it in sports without even understanding that this one factor can be used successfully in our lives as well.

Have a Variety of Coaches

Coaches are like potato chips - you can't have just one. It is very interesting to see that successful teams and athletes have many coaches working in concert to generate top results. In basketball, we have:

1. **Head Coach**: Oversees the big picture of team strategy and implementation. He will create the team style, choose the lineups and manage the game by calling the plays and making substitutions.
2. **Assistant coaches**: Usually three or more to handle the daily tasks of preparing and playing the game. This includes scouting the upcoming opponent and preparing a game plan. They also help analyze the team's performance, looking for ways to improve. During the game, they are tracking player's minutes and advising the head coach on the details of the game action. For instance, they calculate which plays are working, what matchups are beneficial, etc. They also provide the head coach with someone to bounce ideas off.
3. **Development Coaches**: Work with players on their individual skills. This group will include a shooting coach and a position coach (big man or guard coach, for instance) to work on players' individual basketball skills. They usually don't get

involved in the team elements.

4. **Strength and Conditioning Coach**: Trains a player as an athlete. This coach is more of a personal trainer. He works with players to get bigger, faster and stronger, not on basketball technique.
5. **The Trainer**: This is essentially the health coach who treats injuries and advises on health issues in concert with the medical staff.
6. **Sports Psychologist:** His role is to train players in the psychological aspects of competing successfully. For instance, he teaches players how to deal with pressure, keep focused, visualize the action and get in the zone.
7. **Health Professional:** This group will include the nutritionist, physicians of all specialties and other professionals that teach and advise athletes on how to care for their biggest assets, their bodies.

As you can see, these different coaches are all performing a function to help win games. They operate on the big picture team level all the way down to the individual improvement level. Their functions are distinct, complementary and specific to the task at hand. I shared the coaching list for basketball. Football has a much larger team and operates with many more coaches. Even individual athletes have an entourage of coaches. And the better the player, usually the more coaches they have.

Why do sports teams and athletes have so many coaches? What do they know that you don't?

First, we will examine the benefits of coaching. Then we will look at what it means for you in your situation and how you can benefit from ramping up your own coaching staff.

Fast Broke

Benefits of Having a Coach

Coaches benefit athletes in many different ways. I just went over an example of the specific roles of coaches on a staff. As I mentioned, that list was specific to professional basketball. Your coaching staff and their roles will be specific to the sport or task at hand. Clearly there are some roles that are universal and will be filled by specific types of people. For instance, the head coach must be well-rounded and able to see the big picture. The position coaches are more specialized.

The Value of Great Coaching

As I mentioned earlier, athletes view coaching as such an important part of their success that virtually *all athletes* on every level have one or more coaches *at all times*. It is not only in team sports, either. Individual athletes on the highest level, whether it is Tiger Woods, Usain Bolt, Michael Phelps or Serena Williams, have not only one coach but teams of coaches.

What is interesting to note is that the higher the level a player attains, *the more coaching is involved*. You would think that as a player makes it to the pro level, he has it all figured out and needs less coaching. Not so. Athletes understand better than most people that great coaching more than pays for itself. It makes them *more money*.

It is obvious that athletes make their living directly from their performance, so coaching is a natural investment. What about the areas of business and entrepreneurship? Isn't the key to success long hours and hard work? Does coaching matter for them?

Let's look at the value provided by great coaching and see if it sounds like something that would benefit an entrepreneur:

Fast Broke

1. **Leverage other's knowledge and expertise**
   The first reason you get a coach is to learn from someone who knows more about what you are doing than you do. This access will save you years of learning time by teaching you the specialized knowledge you need to succeed.
2. **Leverage other's experience**
   Once you learn the specific information and start taking action, it is typical to get stuck by all of the things that happen in real life that aren't in the textbook. Why spend years making expensive mistake after expensive mistake when you can have an advisor guide you through the landmines you will face?
3. **Provide accountability**
   One of the hardest things to manage in life is distractions. When starting a new business, it is typical to keep doing what you have been doing while you transition. Before you know it, days of inaction turn into weeks and nothing gets done. A coach is really useful to keep you on track with milestones and appointments, providing deadlines to keep. This function is one of the best indicators of success.
4. **Provide structure and resources**
   Most entrepreneurs start businesses on a small budget, doing most of the work themselves. They feel the need to save money by taking on more jobs. Or they may need specialty help that they don't know how to find. Buying and selling real estate needs a variety of people, such as contractors, marketing people, bookkeeping and accounting services, etc. A good coach can provide these people from their own network, or teach you how to screen people, helping eliminate the waste and losses from bad hires.
5. **Provide a different viewpoint**
   One of the most unappreciated elements of coaching is the

outsider's perspective. The reality is that you only see what you can see. If an object is in your blind spot, nothing in the world will help you see it on your own. We all get tripped up by our own perspective and rationalizations at one time or another. It's amazing how the things most hidden from us can be seen instantly by someone else. That's why there is a huge value in being able to bounce ideas off someone else.

6. **Provide inspiration**

    Sometimes it's the simple things that make a huge difference. In every business, there is a point after the fun wears off but before the money rolls in that we just have to put one foot in front of the other and soldier on. These low points happen in every business and often are enough to shut you completely down. It is crucial to have that voice urging you on, providing that push you need. Every athlete knows he can push through obstacles better with someone encouraging him.

7. **Support system**

    There is also a point where you will have a complete breakdown. You know enough to operate when things are working right, but you will eventually hit a spot where the wheels fall off. You have a problem that you have no idea how to solve. You're in over your head; you wiped out your bank account, lost a must-have client or suffered some other catastrophe. You are ready to cash in your chips and bail. Without a support system, you will probably give up on your dreams. After all the effort, the results from all of your work and investment will be lost. You need that backstop to be there and not let you quit.

8. **Helps you overcome fear**

    If you are not terrified during the process of going on your own, then you are not trying hard enough. You will be in the zone of discomfort every day, and the voice of fear is never far away. Remember that courage is not the absence of fear, but the ability of taking action in the face of fear. Having the knowledge that there is someone urging you on at every turn and providing needed assistance during times of a breakdown can make the difference between success and failure.

Remember that information is cheap and possession of it is a poor indicator of future success. The factors that make or break your success are related to your absolute commitment to making it work. That commitment is the entry fee to success. You can't be successful without commitment, but having commitment alone does not guarantee success. The benefits of coaching increase your odds immeasurably. I feel confident saying that without quality coaching, you will have very little chance at success. There are just too many places for things to go bad, too many obstacles and too many missed opportunities. Coaching is the key to overcoming all of those obstacles.

I don't know of one successful person in sports or business who said, "I did it all myself." That is why when athletes make more money, they invest in more coaching. The more complex the situation is, the more value a coach provides.

Entrepreneurs usually think of coaching as a luxury to add as they start getting results. They don't take into account all of the results they lost by not having quality coaching. I believe in studying people who have already had the level of success that you are trying to achieve. So stop trying to be Bill Gates or Warren Buffett. You have much more in common with your favorite athlete.

- He started by learning a skill that he didn't know

- He practiced before he played
- He started small and worked his way up
- Most importantly, he was coached every step of the way

Professional athletes use a system to achieve greatness. Now you can, too.

The Next Step

When Wendy and I started investing, we knew that we had to follow the above steps. Our first step was to figure out what would be our focus. We learned the content at seminars but used coaching to take action. We started in real estate, buying and selling single-family homes. We started with our team first, then built our business processes. It was important to get complete buy-in from everyone before starting.

In the process of learning at seminars, we met a guy who had been flipping houses for several years and was starting out teaching at his own events. He agreed to coach us through the rough spots. When we found our first deal, we ran the details and the offer we wanted to make by him. He also sat down with us and did a dry run so we could practice what to say. It was a good thing we did; in the process of discussing the deal, he made us realize that we were in fact doing a terrible deal. The best coaching advice we received was to not do the deal. If we had, we would have been at risk of a big loss. We learned more from almost screwing it up than we would have had we done a good deal by accident. What a wake-up call that was.

Good coaching saved us a possible $100,000 loss on the first day. With continued coaching and learning, we quickly got up to speed and completed 15 successful deals in the first year, making a nice profit.

Fast Broke

Fast Broke

Epilogue

I have been successful through good times and bad, not because I did everything right, but because I never quit. There were times where I "won the game" even though I didn't do things correctly. For instance, I made money flipping houses because the real estate market was soaring like a rocket. I also "lost games" when I did everything right but was overcome by market forces that were too strong.

But through it all, I kept pushing forward and relied on the winning principles I learned and mastered in sports. If there is one difference between life and sports, it is that the game of life is never over. Even after we are gone, the choices we made live on. So like sports, we are never as good as they say when we are winning and we are never as bad as they say when we are losing.

One of the success keys I will explore in detail next time is the technique of building a structure for success. Without a strong structure, all of the planning in the world is just good ideas. The ability to make it real is what ultimately drives us to success.

To learn more, go to **www.dannyschayes.com**

You will find more resources and information. I look forward to hearing from you.

Fast Broke

Fast Broke

About The Author

Professional basketball is Danny Schayes' family business. His father, Dolph Schayes, was one of the NBA's pioneer stars and named among the 50 Greatest Players in 1996. Danny played in the NBA for 18 years and has trained with five Hall of Fame coaches and seven NBA Coaches of the Year.

After retiring from basketball, Danny became a successful real estate investor with his wife, Wendy. Their business grew from flipping single-family homes to raising equity for large condominium conversion projects around the country. In all, they have bought, developed and sold over 1,000 residential units.

Danny is a sought-after speaker and coach. He is a basketball analyst, having worked for ESPN, Turner Sports and several NBA teams. He is currently a sports economist for Sheridan Hoops and is the Director of Business Optimization for *Intensity* (**www.intensity.com**).

Fast Broke

Danny resides in Arizona with Wendy and their son Logan. To learn more about how Danny can put you on a winning team, check him out at **www.DannySchayes.com.**

www.ingramcontent.com/pod-product-compliance
Lightning Source LLC
Chambersburg PA
CBHW051720170526
45167CB00002B/734